POWER
of
THOUGHTS

POWER
of
THOUGHTS

Tarit Kumar Pal

PUSTAK MAHAL®

Publishers
Pustak Mahal®

Administrative office and sale centre

J-3/16 , Daryaganj, New Delhi-110002
☎ 23276539, 23272783, 23272784 • *Fax:* 011-23260518
E-mail: info@pustakmahal.com • *Website:* www.pustakmahal.com

Branches
Bengaluru: ☎ 080-22234025 • *Telefax:* 080-22240209
E-mail: pustak@airtelmail.in • pustak@sancharnet.in
Mumbai: ☎ 022-22010941, 022-22053387
E-mail: rapidex@bom5.vsnl.net.in
Patna: ☎ 0612-3294193 • *Telefax:* 0612-2302719
E-mail: rapidexptn@rediffmail.com

© **Author**

ISBN 978-81-223-1451-9

Edition: 2013

*Printed at :*Radha Offset, Delhi

"POWER OF THOUGHTS" is dedicated to
my Gurudev late Shri Subhash Chakraborty,
my father late Shri Hemendra Nath Pal
and my mother late Shrimati Sujala Pal

Acknowledgement

My grandson Pradyot Khandai was a constant source of encouragement to me during the entire period of writing this book. Patience and untiring support of my wife Shrimati Urmimala Pal also helped me immensely during the compilation of the book. Along with both of them, I wish to acknowledge with deep sense of gratitude all my elder brothers, sister-in-laws, brother-in-laws, sister, son-in-law, daughter, nephews, nieces and many other well-wishers for their keenness and ever readiness to encourage me and provide me valuable suggestions from time to time.

I would also like to thank inspirational writer madam Nancye Sims. She has been kind enough to permit me to use two of her poems as reference in this book.

Examples related to steel plants and collieries are all factual incidences in IISCO/SAIL, ISP, Burnpur, India. Anecdotes, inspiring stories and quotations which feature in the book are recorded from various sources like excerpts from literatures, extracts from programmes/discussions in T.V and recorded CDs, clippings from news papers, internet survey, lectures of live speakers in different forums etc. The list is exhaustive and since over the period of time I have not maintained the specific details of all the sources, I am unable to express my gratitude to each and every individual.

Prologue

In my early professional days, whenever I was unsuccessful in achieving a desired objective, I used to think that I was a victim of either bad luck or external influences. Those thoughts often caused me to go through cycles of depressions. As time rolled by, horizon of my work periphery also started expanding. Professionally and personally, I started coming across people from different age groups with diverse interests, backgrounds and perceptions about life. The experience I gained in their contacts had positive impact on my thought process. I started feeling more relaxed with enhanced confidence while dealing with different 'situations'. During these periods, especially while in association with some of the outstanding personalities in SAIL, I was awestruck by their visualization of rays of hope even in adverse circumstances, clarity of thought processes while analyzing 'situations' before decision making and firmness in sticking to a goal regardless of inner and outer resistances, discomforts and difficulties.

Realization started sinking in me that one needs to look at every aspects of life from broader perspectives and becoming optimistic, enthusiastic and ever ready to walk extra miles to make things happen is the key to success. Subsequently, on retrospection, I was able to reason out within myself that most of the failures and 'period of depressions' that I had gone through in the past were caused by my own thoughts and beliefs at that point in time (nothing external).

I had gone through successes as well as failures. During rough times, whenever I had been pushed back to the wall, the above experiences, inspiring stories and events always reminded me of my strengths and stimulated my motivation to face the reality with rejuvenated spirit.

After retirement from the professional life, while recapitulating, the following realizations spontaneously surfaced in my mind:

(a) Thoughts and attitudes play important roles in determining successes, failures and levels of human performances.

(b) Thought accepted as truth is belief. It makes one feel that whatever he/she hopes for will actually happen and spurs him/her to face reality.

(c) Nothing happens of its own. One has to make things happen.

(d) To keep ever learning is the way to move forward. It builds confidence and ensures growth. No learning goes to waste.

(e) Knowledge, conviction, courage to face problems, avoiding delays and fixing priorities are essential requisites for good decision making.

(f) Life offers plenty of options to every individual.

When the idea of documenting the above for the benefit of the budding youngsters started playing in my mind, I was not sure about how to go ahead. The following anecdote finally gave me the confidence and inspired me to put pen to paper and 'complete the documentation' in the form of the book – POWER OF THOUGHTS. In the book, in some cases, to highlight certain observations and realizations I have drawn references from history and established stories.

When Swami Vivekananda was delivering a specific lecture in a hall, someone from the audience stood up and said, "All these are mere words which have no effects." Vivekananda reacted and called that man a fool and uttered few strong words towards him. The man got excited and was about to hit Vivekananda. Physically stopping him, Vivekananda said, "Look, this is the effect of words. So, words have effects if listened carefully and understood well." I am sure the "words" of this book will benefit the youngsters in their search for a successful/meaningful life.

Tarit Kumar Pal (tkpal3@yahoo.com)
Q. 71, B. P. Township. Patuli,
Kolkata – 700094. Mobile 09832179193

Index

Chapter One

Importance of Thoughts

Thoughts play important roles in human life. Plato said, "Take charge of your thoughts. You can do what you will with them." With the exception of the existence of the elements of nature, everything that exists in this world is created by human thoughts.

Human mind produce thoughts which are reflected in the feelings of individuals. Through monitoring of feelings, it is possible to identify one's thoughts at a particular moment; this enables him/her to exercise power to bring about changes in his/her thinking (if required).

1.1 We live in a human mind made world

Lord Buddha said, "We live in a mind made world." The main function of mind is to produce thoughts. Poet John Milton said, "The mind is its own place, and in itself can make an heaven of hell and hell of an heaven..." The above aptly describe the tremendous power of mind. However, to most of the common people who do not put in much of efforts to understand how the mind works, it still continues to be the least understood faculty of human soul. It is something one cannot see, touch or measure with any scientific gadgets, yet its effects are felt – through expressions, actions and behaviour. It works nonstop and is an inseparable companion of human being.

Like muscles 'mind' stretches or shrinks respectively depending on how much or how little one makes use of it.

It is a common knowledge that knives are used for various purposes. A doctor uses a knife to operate a patient for his/her good, a villain uses a knife to 'kill' or harm his/her victim and a house wife uses a knife for her cooking preparations. The good and bad are not in the knives; it is in their use. Similarly, good and bad are not in human being; they are caused by different thoughts produced by the mind.

'Mind' becomes one's best asset when he/she produces good thoughts and nourishes it. It however can turn into his/her worst enemy when he/she lets himself/herself produce damaging thoughts.

Like the 'foundations' are responsible for the stability of buildings, the 'mind' is responsible for the stability of human being. Famous West Indian cricketer Sir Vivian Richards while corroborating the above said in his cricketing language, "Batting isn't like a house, where the foundation starts at the bottom and the building progresses upwards. Here the foundation starts at the top (in the mind). If your mind is doing well, you will do well." (The Telegraph, Kolkata 9.6.2013).

'Mind' cannot differentiate between negation and affirmation. When one constantly thinks of not doing some particular thing, the mind gets the message of 'doing that particular thing' and tries to bring that into existence. The following Buddhist tale is relevant in the above context.

A Buddhist monk went to his master one day and asked for some guidelines to meditate during a period of three days of absence. The master replied, "During these three days you can think of anything other than monkeys." After three days when the disciple went to meet his master, the master asked him about the last three day's experience. The disciple replied, "I cannot understand what happened. All these three days I could not think of anything other than the monkeys." This is a reality in human life and it explains the failure of many people whose thoughts are concentrated more on what they don't want rather than on what they want. Energy spent in thinking, talking or worrying about what one does not want always keeps that alive.

Great philosopher Carl Jung was spot on when he said, "What you desist, persists." The solution lies in replacing the thought of what one does not want with thought of what he/she wants.

1.2 Creation of thoughts and feelings

Thoughts are created either by the external stimuli (information from outside also referred as thought impulses) which enter one's mind through the organs of senses – seeing, tasting, touching, hearing and smelling or through emergence of response when the impression cabinet in the subconscious mind (discussed in chapter two) is stimulated by an external stimulus. Major parts of human thoughts however are determined by what one perceives through the former. Out of the five human senses mentioned above, 'seeing' and 'hearing' processes as much as eighty percent of the received stimuli to produce thoughts.

Thoughts cause feelings. If one thinks of an unhappy incident of the past, he/she immediately starts feeling unhappy again. Similarly, if one thinks of a happy incident of the past, he/she starts feeling happy while recollecting the event in the mental picture.

One feels bad only when his/her thoughts make him/her feel so. And unless and until he/she makes conscious efforts to change thoughts to feel better, he/she will continue to invite more circumstances that will make him/her feel bad. It is impossible to feel good and at the same time have unhappy/bad thoughts.

It is said that more than 50,000 thoughts make invasion in human mind like powerful volcanoes in one single day. To single out each and every one of these thoughts is very difficult. However, it is possible to know from one's feelings (emotions) what types of thought he/she is thinking at a particular moment. Emotion therefore is a valuable tool that instantly tells the type of thought one is involved in.

Since one chooses his thoughts and he/she is the one who feels the effects, he/she can always exercise power to consciously influence his/her thoughts.

Following his/her thought patterns, at any point of time if one realizes that his/her current thought is unlikely to yield desired end result when it manifests, he/she always has the option to change his/her thinking.

I.3 Attitude/action sprouts from thought

With the exception of the existence of the elements of nature, everything that exists in this world is created by human thoughts.

Thoughts are the primary cause of everything. Whatever one sees, feels and experiences in this world are the effects.

All inventions in this world are creations which began with thoughts from which paths were found and they manifested from invisible into the visible. Thoughts exist in reality as dynamic waves whose sole purpose is to carry out the intent of the thinker.

Thoughts have the following two key parameters:

(a)   A frequency of vibration corresponding to the intent, and

(b)   A magnitude corresponding to the amount of desire associated with it.

It is said, "You define your personality, physical attributes and behaviour. You are the one who can create or change your thoughts and your beliefs. And your beliefs create what you experience as life."

In the biography of Thomas Alva Edison written by his son, a freezing December night of 1914 has been recalled. Unfruitful experiments on a ten year project on nickel - iron - alkaline storage battery had put Edison aged sixty seven years, on a tight rope. He was still solvent only because of profits he earned from his other ventures. On that evening, Edison's factory worth few million dollars was on fire. The intensity of fire was so high that even fire companies from eight surrounding towns could not douse it before everything was destroyed. When the devastating flame was in rampage, Edison saw his son and asked, "Where is your mother? Call her to see the spectacle. She is never going to see anything like this in her entire life again."

His wife came and saw the catastrophe. Next day, during the morning walk when the couple was moving through the remains of the factory, Edison told his wife, "There is great value in disaster. All our mistakes are burnt up. Thank God, we can start anew." This brought back the lady's lost smile and lit up her dull face. He called all his colleagues and made an incredible announcement, "We are rebuilding!" He further explained, "We can always make capital out of a disaster. We have just cleared out a bunch of old rubbish. We will build bigger and better on the ruins." Three months later he invented Phonograph.

Thoughts are like seeds; attitude and actions sprout from them.

1.4 Thoughts in isolation and silence

Thinking in isolation and in silence has tremendous effect in human life. It has been discussed earlier that since more than 50,000 thoughts pass through one's mind in a day, it is difficult to single out each and every thought.

Thinking in isolation gives one a chance to single out a thought from all the thoughts and give enough time for its concrete crystallization while other thoughts are kept away. Silence makes room for introspection and enables one to bring clarity to thoughts.

A farmer once lost his watch in a barn. It was one of his assets with lots of sentimental values attached to it. Having failed in his search to locate the watch, he engaged a group of children playing outside the barn with a promise to reward whoever could recover it for him. All the enthusiastic children rushed inside the barn. But after exhausting all their efforts, they surrendered and expressed their inability to locate it.

Finally, when the farmer lost all hopes and was getting ready to move towards his home, a small boy approached him. The boy said, "Sir, give me a chance to go inside the barn once more. This time I shall go alone." The farmer agreed. The boy went inside, and after some time came back with the watch. The farmer asked the boy surprisingiy, "How did you manage to find it?" The boy replied, "I just sat quietly in all silence. After some time when I heard a ticking sound, I moved in that direction and located the watch."

In isolation and in silence, one can always concentrate better on a particular object. The mental process of focusing a thought intensely and extensively on a particular object, in a quiet environment without any external disturbance is known as manifestation meditation. It is a habit which can be developed through practice.

1.5   Thoughts freeze achievement level

Dale Carnegie was once asked to tell in short the most important lesson he had ever learned. He said, "The most important lesson I have ever learned is the stupendous importance of what we think. If I knew what you think, I would know what you are, for your thoughts make you what you are. By changing our thoughts we can change our lives."

All the actions that one sees in this world, all the movements in human society, all the works that one has around him/her are simply the display of thoughts, the manifestation of the will of mankind.

Man or woman cannot achieve anything without first conceiving it in thought. Carl Lewis, the champion Olympic athlete of U.S.A was spot on when he said, "If you are running down the track of life thinking it is impossible to break life's records, those thoughts have a funny way of sinking into your feet."

Thoughts determine one's level of achievement. One therefore should always think high and set targets at higher levels (high enough so that he/she has to stretch but not so high that he/she may break) to extract the best in him/her and also to ensure that even if he/she fails to get where he/she set his/her mind to, he/she still remains pretty close.

Former British Prime Minister Benjamin Disraeli very rightly said, "Nurture your mind with great thoughts for you will never go any higher than you think."

1.6   Various types of human thoughts

Whether one understands it, believes it, realizes it or not, he/she is always thinking something except when he/she is asleep. Since every individual has his own mental world and own mode of thinking, different thoughts are produced in the process. These thoughts can broadly be classified as 'essential thoughts', 'nonessential thoughts', 'negative thoughts', 'positive thoughts' etc.

Essential thoughts are mostly related to one's needs and responsibilities and are generally connected to personal, family or professional life on routine basis.

'Essential thoughts' become 'nonessential' when they are repeated again and again. Thoughts on past or future are also nonessential in nature since one cannot do anything about the past and nobody knows what is going to happen in the future.

Nonessential thoughts consume lots of valuable time and weaken one's ability to concentrate. They are the basic cause of worry and anxiety which drains one's energy like a leak from a tank.

Any form of obsessive thinking which does not have the potential to yield anything worthwhile in the long run other than to make one suffer, constitute negative thought.

Negative thoughts are self destructive. They are a form of inner pollution that needs to be cleansed to make the mind a more efficient tool.

Positive thoughts are always directed towards finding the best possible way to respond to different situations in life.

Positive thought helps one to overcome 'obsession' and 'confusion' and makes him/her feel relaxed and take charge of life under all circumstances.

Thoughts are also classified as violent, destructive, subtle or spiritual depending on the mood and intent of the thinker.

Thoughts move and pass from one individual to another. A person of powerful thoughts can readily influence people of weaker thoughts.

1.7 Why positive thoughts are desired?

Human mind can be compared to wireless machines. A positive mind emits harmonious waves of thoughts, which travel with lightning speed and echo in the mind of others. In contrast, a negative mind sends out discordant thoughts. Negative thoughts such as hatred, lust, jealousy and selfishness produce distorted images in the mind with confusions and causes clouding of understanding, intellect and loss of memory.

Zig Zagler said, "Positive thinking will let you do everything better than negative thinking will." Positive thought always have beneficial effects. It harms no one and is a way of seeing life and doing things with optimism, enthusiasm, resoluteness and assertiveness.

There was a giant called Goliath. He was frightening and tormenting the inhabitants of a village. One day a shepherd boy named David visited his brothers in that village. Having come to know the extent of panic the giant had created amongst the villagers, he curiously asked his brothers, "Why don't you all stand against the giant and drive him out?" His petrified brothers replied in chorus, "He is a very big and strongly built fellow." David shot back, "We must then make a specific strategy to attack him." David's positive thinking led him to adapt an unconventional strategy to attack the giant with stones and sling for which Goliath was not prepared. Eventually they killed the giant.

Positive thinking always pushes people to directly face adverse situations/problems instead of trying to escape from the reality or fall into the traps of negativity through inaction.

When negative thoughts creep in the mind, it starts poisoning the life within and slowly starts making dents into one's confidence, integrity and God gifted abilities. They are not to be nurtured.

Negative thoughts always drain one's energy. With negative thinking, one

(a)   develops a sense of insecurity, has no imagination, plan or vision,

(b)   loses 'motivation' and 'focus',

(c)   is unproductive and always suffers from fear and frustration,

(d)   is directionless and often sees problems and faults everywhere.

Negative thoughts are generally related to past events and experiences. While travelling in a taxi, a passenger once tapped the driver from the back to ask him something. As an immediate reaction, the driver became panicky. Out of fear, he lost control over the taxi, nearly hit another car, missed a truck and went off the road before stopping in front of a roadside shop. After a pause the driver screamed, "You scared me to death." When the passenger apologized for tapping him from behind, the driver replied, "Sorry. It is not your fault. Today is my first day as a taxi driver. For the past ten years I have been ferrying only dead bodies in a van."

1.8   Determined thoughts and creativity

Determined positive thoughts make people creative and committed towards tasks on hand.

Creativity need not necessarily be associated with original idea only. Every time one comes up with an idea to improve even some part of his/her work or find newer, faster and cheaper way to do a job, he/she is said to be creative.

Determined thoughts make people believe that whatever they hope for will actually happen. It is relevant to quote Mahatma Gandhi in this context. He said, "If I have the belief that I can do it, I shall surely acquire the capacity to do it even if I may not have it at the beginning."

Since his youth, 'Demosthenes the Great' had a burning desire to excel in public speaking. However, because of his tendency to stammer, he was often hissed, hooted and taunted whenever he had gone for public speaking. One day, after being laughed out of a forum for his sobering and panting efforts at speech, he felt devastated and was walking around a port. Noticing him, a local actor approached him and after few exchange of words, asked him to recite a passage from an identified literature. During recital, whenever Demosthenes faltered, the actor would himself repeat the same passages with full expressions of feelings, emotions and gestures. Demosthenes was charmed, inspired and influenced by the eloquent speech of the actor.

26

Subsequently, for improving work on his voice, modulations, gestures, cadence and logic, he started practicing speeches in isolation in a newly built underground shelter. To avoid meeting people so that he could devote more time on practice, he shaved off half of his head followed by shaving off the other half. After sometime, when he felt more at ease in speaking, he started reciting speeches while running up the hills and followed it up by sea shore oratory against and over the breaking of waves. He even went to the extent of putting pebbles under his tongue and enunciating over the roaring surf. His determined thoughts to excel in public speaking backed by committed actions eventually drove him not only to become a great name to be reckoned with in Greece, he went on to become one of the greatest orators and a statesman of his time.

To bring about improvements, people with determined thoughts are not afraid of challenging the 'status quo'.

Even though for ages people considered running a mile race under four minutes as impossible, Roger Bannister thought it otherwise. He not only practiced hard but also constantly visualized achieving the feat himself with so much of intensity that his mind and body got tuned to make it happen. Eventually he became the first man in the history to achieve the feat on 6th of May 1954.

1.9 Necessity of monitoring of thoughts

It has been referred in section 1.2 that whenever one understands that his/her particular thought is not likely to yield the desired end result when it manifests, he/she has the option to erase and replace the thought with thought of his/her own desire. This however does not happen as a natural process. Generally, when one fails to get what he/she wants, his/her mind quickly creates a limiting belief like, 'an injustice have been done to me', 'I am unfortunate', 'it is not for me' etc.

Limiting beliefs arise either because of one's lack of confidence and sufficient knowledge about a task on hand or because of his/her hesitation to introspect. They are progress breakers and are usually well hidden in one's belief system. They can be got rid of only when one admits that he/she carries them in his/her belief system. The above calls for monitoring of thought patterns (attitude).

In aviation, the word attitude means the angle at which a plane meets the wind, irrespective of whether the plane is climbing, descending or its wings are level with horizon. The pilot who fails to monitor and take responsibility for the attitude of his aircraft often lands in serious trouble. The key lies in monitoring and taking control.

In human life too, monitoring and taking control of one's thought pattern (attitude) is very important. Monitoring enables one to be aware of the thought patterns and decide which type of thought he/she has to focus on so that he/she can condition the mind as per his/her desire.

After monitoring, one can evaluate with a calm mind and respond to the situation appropriately so that his/her energy and time is put in the right direction. Impulsive reactions often lead to disastrous results.

1.10   Thoughts create circumstances

Ex. Chief of Tata, Ratan Tata said, "Ups and downs in life are very important to keep us going, because a straight line even in an E. C. G. means we are not alive." One can always get shaken by certain events in life, but that does not stop him/her from thinking positive and taking actions to move forward again. Irrespective of what happens to him/her or wherever he/she is, one always has the option to choose and start afresh (refer section 1.3), if necessary, he/she can even give a new direction to life. Adolf Hitler who made the quotes, "If you win, you need not have to explain" & "If you lose, you should not be there to explain" wanted to make painting his career. However when his application for admission to Viennese Academy of Arts was rejected, he diverted his concentration and focus and eventually gave a new direction to life.

Jessica Cox (refer section 8.5, chapter eight) flies aircraft in spite of not having both her hands since birth. Doug Landis (refer section 8.5, chapter eight) excels in mouth art in spite of his body being paralyzed from neck below. No situation is absolutely hopeless. Human mind make them so. Ratan Tata, the ex. chief of Tata Group rightly said, "None can destroy iron, but its own dust can! Likewise, none can destroy a person, but his own mindset can."

In the journey of life, thoughts and beliefs determine which path one takes, what he/she looks back at, and what he/she looks forward to. If one persistently thinks and picturize 'fear' or 'hopeless situation', the subconscious mind (discussed in chapter two) gets programmed and creates the 'fear' or 'hopeless situation' for him/her.

To move forward in life, one has to think positive all the time. The following quote from Martin Luther King Jr. is very relevant in this context. He said, "If you can't fly, then run. If you can't run, then walk. If you can't walk, then crawl. But whatever you do, you have to keep moving forward."

Thoughts create circumstances. The great statesman of Victorian England, Benjamin Disraeli's maiden speech was very badly received in the House of Commons in 1937 and ended abruptly when he was hissed, silenced and shouted down by the other members of the parliament. Before getting down from the dais, he said, "Though I sit down now, the time will come when you will hear of me." Subsequently, instead of brooding over the incidence, he continued to think positive and work harder with determination. Eventually, he went on to become the Prime Minister of England and that too for two separate terms.

Later Benjamin Franklin was spontaneous in saying, "We are not creatures of circumstances; we are creators of circumstances."

Chapter Two

Thought Condition Attitude

Thoughts form the basics of human perception, habit and attitude. Attitude has the potential to take one either forward or backward and is influenced by the operation of conscious mind and the subconscious mind. There are techniques to influence the subconscious mind with desired thoughts to bring about a conscious change in attitude.

2.1 Thought/perception/way of life

While thoughts are created by external stimuli (thought impulses) which enter one's mind through the organs of senses – seeing, tasting, touching, hearing and smelling, perception is formed arising out of observation, interpretation or a mental image that one holds with regard to events, conditions or circumstances. Out of many factors like experiences, beliefs, memory, people, situations, etc., beliefs and experiences have maximum influence towards the formation of perception.

Perception reflects in likes, dislikes and lifestyles of individuals

When Alexander the Great set his mind to conquer India and was getting ready for the venture, he was upset and deeply hurt to notice the indifference of one of his very close friends who was purposely avoiding him for quite some time. The day before he set out for his mission, Alexander went to meet his friend sunbathing in a nearby place. Meeting his friend, Alexander was excited and started narrating the plans of expansion of his empire. To his friend's only query "what next?" he went on replying that he would accumulate lots of wealth, become a famous monarch and get his name immortalized in history. Continuing, he said that finally he would settle down in his home town and peacefully relax for the rest of his life. At that point, his friend spontaneously replied that he was exactly doing what Alexander planned to do after fulfilling his goals in life. He further said that he believed in relaxation all the time and resigned to his fate believing that whatever had to happen would happen. It was their difference in 'perceptions' which prompted Alexander the Great and his friend to adapt different approaches towards life.

Perception differs in each perspective. This is illustrated best through the expressions of feelings of a deaf - who says, "For all of you, I am a deaf, but for me all of you are dumb."

Different perceptions also form from the same events, conditions or circumstances. There was a man who was addicted to drinking alcohol. He led a very disturbed family as well as professional life. Under the influence of alcohol, he often caused chaos in the family. Whenever he was asked about the reason for such behaviour, he would reply, "I drink to forget the miseries and challenges of life. Drinking makes me feel as if I am on cloud nine." This man was an escapist who was not mentally prepared to face the realities of life and often saw pitfalls rather than opportunities in life.

He had two sons. When they grew up, one of them became 'alcohol addicted' and did not progress much in life. The other son however led a very happy and prosperous life. On being asked about their different lifestyles, the alcohol addicted son would say, "I have emulated whatever I had seen my father doing since my childhood." The other son however would say, "As a young kid I saw my father doing all wrong things under the influence of alcohol. So I made up my mind not to follow his footsteps."

Growing in the same environment, the brothers developed different perceptions about life.

Based on perceptional difference, mankind is broadly classified into three categories:

(a)   Those who want to make things happen,

(b)   Those who watch things happen and

(c)   Those who wonder what is happening?

(a)   Those who want to make things happen

Einstein said "Nothing happens unless something moves." This group is a staunch believer of the above philosophy. They utilize their 'thinking' as well as 'doing work' capacity to the fullest. They plan, set goals and are persistently focused to condition their desire to come to existence. They are the cause of their own situations and they believe more in changing themselves rather than changing their circumstances. They have the courage and stamina to face and conquer adversity with 'never say quit' resolve.

(b)   Those who watch things happen

They are not at all ambitious as a result they seldom take initiatives to create opportunities to bring about any major changes in life. They mostly resign to their fate, which grant them the life they deserve that too if and when it decides to do so. Incidences happening around them attract their attention to such an extent that they often get distracted and fail to address more important things in life. Because of lack of desire to live a fulfilled life, their 'potential' often remain underutilized.

(c)   Those who wonder what is happening

They do not look for opportunities and often don't even recognize them when those surface. They don't prepare themselves and are not at all updated with what is happening around them. Only occasionally they wake up and start wondering about what is happening around. Because they lack in conviction, they do not take any positive stand in life and their 'potential' remain unexplored.

Summing up his observations on human characteristics, poet Robert Frost rightly said, "The world is full of willing people, some willing to work, and the rest willing to let them."

2.2 Formation of habits and attitudes

Formation of a habit does not take very long time. One just needs to think about something a few times and consciously put it into action. The more one repeats the action, the less conscious he/she becomes of the initial thought and finally a time comes when he/she does not know why he/she is doing whatever he/she is doing. All his/her actions become automatic and form habit. He/she is reminded of the initial thought only during introspection.

Once the habits are formed, individuals display spontaneous actions and reactions under external stimulation. Psychiatrist Jung termed this readiness of 'psyche' to act or react in certain ways as 'attitude'. Thoughts therefore directly contribute towards the development of human attitude.

Attitude is a complex mental state that dictates human responses involving beliefs, feelings, values, dispositions etc. It is a very powerful mechanism working twenty four hours a day for good or for bad and has the potential to take one either forward or backward. Consciously inculcating a system of harnessing this great force therefore is of utmost importance.

R. Swindoll said, "The longer I live, the more I realize the impact of attitude on life.....we cannot change our past....we cannot change the fact that people will act in a certain way. We cannot change the inevitable. The only thing we can do is play on the string we have, and that is our attitude. I am convinced that life is ten percent of what happens to me and ninety percent of how I react to it. And so it is with you.....we are in charge of our attitudes."

To know more about the mechanism of how attitude is formed and its impact on human life, understanding the functioning of the human brain and operation of the 'mind' is essential.

2.3 Human brain and its functions

Human brain is an electrochemical organ which constantly emanates an oscillating electrical voltage of the order of few millionths of a volt. These impulses are called brain waves and are measured in cycles per second.

Depending on the magnitude of the brain waves, human mind is divided into four states.

For most of the 'waking hours', one generally is in beta state where the brain radiates waves at the rate of 14 cycles per second and above. In this state –

(a)   one has mental alertness and high level of concentration,

(b)   the mind is sharp and focused and makes connections quickly,

(c)   the mind is engaged mostly in thinking, reasoning and problem solving,

(d)   one easily primes to do work which requires full attention.

As the brain waves slow down to between 8 and 13 cycles per second, one enters the alpha state of mind. In this state –

(a)   door between conscious mind and subconscious mind is opened,

(b)   one can easily access the storage of information in the memory,

(c)   one's awareness expands, mind and body gets relaxed, fear vanishes and fresh creative energy begins to flow.

With further lowering of the brain waves, measuring between 4 to 7 cycles/second, one is said to be in theta state. The border line between the alpha and the theta state is the doorway to the super conscious mind. Going deeper into relaxation, one enters this state where the brain activity slows down almost to the point of sleep, but not quite. This is the barely conscious state just before sleeping and just after waking. In this state –

(a) one is open to ideas and can access wisdom that lies beyond the border of normal awareness,

(b) one is very positive and vibrant.

When the brain waves further slow down to less than 4 cycles per second, one is said to be in a dream state or delta state. In this state, one is either in deep sleep or totally unconscious.

Each individual experiences the Theta level for a fleeting moment every night before the mind dips down from the Beta level of awareness (awake state), passes through the Alpha state and ends up in the Delta state (where consciousness of self is totally lost, and even dreams do not occur. When dreaming, a sense of self is necessary and the mind has to go back up to the Theta or Alpha state).

There is also a Gamma brain wave corresponding to 40 cycles per second and above. Though an integral part of the brain, gamma waves play only a supporting role.

All the above mentioned five brain wave frequencies are normally present together in the brain. However, the most dominating frequency determines what shall be called 'the current state' of the brain waves.

Beta is the so-called conscious level of mind. It is the primary part of human brain involved in the thinking process. Alpha and Theta form the subconscious and super conscious regions of the mind's operation respectively. Delta is the unconscious region of thought activity. These states form the spectrum of mind operation.

2.4 Human mind and its operations

Human mind operates through conscious mind, subconscious mind and the super conscious mind. They are all endowed with distinct attributes and powers.

Conscious mind

The conscious mind receives all the thought impulses the environment supplies, through the five human senses – seeing, tasting, touching, hearing and smelling. It has the ability to apply logic and reasoning to the received thought impulses and filter them if necessary. After application of logic and reasoning and subsequent filtration, the conscious mind decides whether it will reject a thought impulse or process and funnel it on to the subconscious mind.

Subconscious mind

Subconscious mind basically is a data bank. It cannot do anything of its own. It is responsible for all the involuntary actions one is born with like breathing, digestion etc. and programmes like walking, talking, changing of gears while driving a car, peddling bicycles etc. which one creates subsequently.

Thoughts repeatedly funneled through the conscious mind become impressions and get programmed in the subconscious mind. These impressions are stored in the subconscious mind in an organized manner as different retrievable memory cabinets as mentioned below.

(a) *Identification and interpretation cabinet:* it identifies and interprets the nature of impressions received and stores them accordingly.

(b) *Give and take cabinet*: it maintains all types of 'give and take' accounts. It often tries to settle scores with others whenever and wherever opportunity permits.

(c) *Like and dislike cabinet:* it stores impressions on likes and dislikes and on stimulation sends impulses back to conscious mind.

(d) *Instincts and desire cabinet:* it is the storage of all desires and instincts.

(e) *Temperamental characteristic cabinet:* it stores the temperamental characteristics of individuals.

There is also an intelligence cabinet. It modifies impressions based on the knowledge stored there in. Actions and reactions of these impression cabinets on external stimulation directly control human behaviour.

On external stimulation, one starts responding through the above five deep rooted impressions and the final response emerge through the intelligence cabinet. Impressions mixed with emotions always respond first. This explains why sometimes one starts getting emotional even though he/she does not want to feel so.

Operation of conscious mind and subconscious mind

When one breathes on intention, then the conscious mind is in charge. However when he/she is breathing without being conscious of the breathing process, the subconscious mind is in charge.

Conscious and subconscious mind can also operate simultaneously as explained below. While learning to drive a car, because of being engrossed and focused on the different moves involved in driving, initially one is unable to hold any conversation with others. However over a period of time, when all his/her actions and reactions to driving becomes spontaneous, he/she can drive effortlessly while holding conversation (even talk on mobile phones) with others. This becomes possible because through repetitive practice, the conscious driving efforts get transferred and programmed in the subconscious mind and the conscious mind becomes free. This enables the conscious mind and the subconscious mind to operate independently.

Conscious mind/Subconscious mind/Iceberg in ocean

In an ocean, only a small portion of iceberg (around 10 %) floats on the surface, while the balance major portion remains underneath. Likewise, the smaller part of human mind known as conscious mind works on the surface while the bigger part known as subconscious mind works from underneath. Like the submerged part of an iceberg, the subconscious mind is also very powerful.

Conscious mind has a short time memory. It can process about 1 - 3 events at a time and 40 bits of information per second. The subconscious mind however, has a long term memory and can process more than thousand events at a time and four billions of information per second.

Super conscious mind

It is often observed that when one is involved in a conversation or listens to discussions, some ideas or inspirations leap into his/her mind even though they have no direct relevance to the conversation and the discussion of reference. And those ideas and inspirations ultimately come out to be the exact input that he/she needed at that point in time to move forward in life. Here the super conscious mind is at work. Super conscious mind contains within itself the possibility as well as the probability of creating anything and everything that is conceived by the 'mind'. It comes into play automatically when one has clarity of thoughts about what he/she wants and is calm and confident about his/her ability to achieve it. Apart from making access to all the information stored in the subconscious mind, it has the ability to access the experiences, knowledge, ideas and intelligence that had ever existed, or will ever exist. 'Hunch' or 'inspiration' arising out of super conscious mind is timed and dated; they warrant immediate attention and follow up actions.

When the conscious mind sends repetitive command to the subconscious mind, messages get programmed in the subconscious mind and super conscious mind starts to make things happen.

2.5 Formation of positive and negative attitude

Thoughts repeatedly passed through the conscious mind to the subconscious mind get ingrained into one's system and become programmed impressions in the subconscious mind. On external stimulation, these impressions respond spontaneously through one's thoughts, speeches, actions and behaviour. The readiness of psyche to act or react in a certain way under external stimulation is termed as attitude.

An old man was once asked by his grandson to explain why some people have positive attitude while others have negative attitude. The old man said, "A continuous battle goes inside every human being. You can call it a battle between two wolves. Wolf no. 1 represents anger, envy, jealousy, sorrow, regret, greed, self-pity, arrogance, guilt, resentment, inferiority complex, lies, false pride, feelings of superiority, ego etc. Wolf no. 2 represents joy, peace, love, hope, serenity, humility, kindness, benevolence, empathy, generosity, truth, compassion, faith etc." The grandson suddenly interrupted and asked, "Which wolf finally wins?" The grandfather simply replied, "The one which is fed more."

Positive attitude or negative attitude is formed depending on the dominance of the positive or negative thoughts respectively that one permits to occupy his/her mind.

Environment and the people one keeps company with have marked influence on his/her attitude. If what one hears, sees and reads is always negative, he/she accepts this as the standard way of thinking and behaving. Similarly when what one hears, sees and reads is always positive, he/she accepts this as the standard way of thinking and behaving.

Positive attitude do not always guarantee success but it makes one anticipate happiness, joy and successful outcome of every action under all circumstances. It inspires people to face the realities of life with an open mind. Like a parachute, human mind works best when open.

Negative attitude damages one's confidence to such an extent that he/she often feels that situations surrounding him/her are not only out of control, they are also not retrievable. It makes one believe that whatever bad had happened in the past will continue to happen for the rest of the periods in his/her life; he/she starts seeing the future in his/her past. It has a serious negative impact. It is like driving a car forward looking at the rear view mirror. Sooner or later, it will result into a crash. With negative attitude one's potential is never fully utilized.

Positive and negative attitude make a lot of difference in human life. W. Clement Stone said, "There is little difference in people, but that little difference makes a big difference. The little difference is attitude. The big difference is whether it is positive or negative."

2.6   Positive attitude always create victors

Everything in this universe has a polar opposite – black/white, positive/negative, in/out, day/night, love/fear, success/failure, loss/gain etc. Choice rests with every individual to either look at the brighter or at the darker side of life.

Positive attitude makes people concentrate on the brighter side of life. By concentrating on the possibilities, they make things happen whereas people with negative attitude focus more on what is impossible until what they see is impossibility.

There was a man who always used to be in positive mood. Whenever people approached him for advice, he would tell them to look at the brighter side of the situation. When asked how he could be in such positive state of mind all the time, he would reply,

"(a)   early morning, when I get up from bed, I have two choices before me – good mood and bad mood, I choose the former.

43

(b)   When something bad happens, between the two options before me – to become a victim or learn from it, I choose the latter.

(c)   When someone comes to me complaining, between the two options in front of me – to accept the complaint or point out the positive side of it, I choose the latter."

One day this man had a fall from a height and met with a serious accident. After long hours of surgery and weeks of intensive care, he was released from the hospital with steel rod placed at his back. When he was asked what did go through his mind as the injury took place, he said,

"(a)   the first thing that went through my mind was the well being of my soon-to-be born child.

(b)   laying on the ground, I then remembered that I had two choices before me – either to live or die. I choose the former.

(c)   the paramedics were great. They kept on telling me that I was going to be fine, even though I could read it from the faces of the doctors and nurses that they were doubtful about my survival.

(d)   a big burly nurse asked me if I was allergic to anything (obviously meaning medicine). When I replied that I was allergic to 'Gravity', the whole team burst into laughter. Over their laughter, I told them, I am choosing to live. Operate me as if I am alive, not dead."

The man finally survived and lived happily thereafter, not only because of the skills of the doctors and the care of the nurses but also because of his amazing attitude.

Circumstances cannot always be chosen in life, but one can certainly choose his/her attitude. It is the attitude which makes one feel a victor or a vanquished. Positive attitude always makes people feel victors.

2.7 Maintaining harmony within mind

Subconscious mind always expresses what the conscious mind has impressed on it. It submits to the impressions and decisions of the conscious mind with total compliance without making any argument or choice. It cannot differentiate between good and bad as well as right and wrong. It acts involuntarily and effortlessly as an automatic response to external stimuli. It is very responsive to emotions and has a tendency to emulate what it is being fed most and the environment it is most familiar with.

On external stimulation the subconscious mind proceeds to work automatically on the 'impressions' made upon it even without the awareness of the conscious mind. The conscious mind however notices the 'effect' soon and starts its action. If the conscious mind reasons against the 'effect' and cannot accept it, it will send conflicting signal that will undo the work of the subconscious mind. It is therefore mandatory that the conscious and the subconscious mind are in harmony otherwise it will be impossible for one to achieve a goal no matter what it may be.

Emotions are messages sent by the subconscious mind back to the conscious mind in order to notify a person about 'something'. Since emotions are triggered by the subconscious mind, apparently it appears to be impossible to control them. However, knowing that the conscious mind processes thoughts, which are the primary trigger for emotions, one can convince the conscious mind to send appropriate messages to the subconscious mind so that both are in harmony. When both are in harmony, the mind becomes more creative and productive. With lesser harmony between the two, the entire mind as a whole collapse and fail to function properly.

Nature has so built the mankind that if desired they can exercise absolute control over the materials which reach their subconscious mind through the conscious mind. This however does not always happen in reality, mainly because as an adult, one often spends more time subconsciously reacting rather than consciously creating desired messages in the subconscious storage.

2.8 Changing of attitude is possible

Motivational author Robert Collier said, "It is only through your conscious mind that you can reach your subconscious mind. Your conscious mind is the porter at the door, the watchman at the gate. It is the conscious mind that the subconscious mind looks for all its impressions."

From above and also from section 2.7, it is clear that by repeatedly and consciously feeding more of desired thoughts to the conscious mind, one can impress the subconscious mind to bring about a desired change in attitude. This is where thought monitoring (refer section 1.9) comes into play. After monitoring, if the thoughts are found to be negative, one can consciously shut off the flow of negative thought impulses and voluntarily replace them with positive thoughts of desire.

Napoleon Hill specifically said, "Positive and negative emotions cannot occupy the mind at the same time. One or the other must dominate. It is your responsibility to make sure that positive emotions constitute the dominating influence in your mind."

There was a benevolent king who was very knowledgeable and very caring towards his subjects. People from distant places used to come to him for positive advice. Once a man came to him and said, "King! I get angry quite often. How can I control my anger?" The king listened to all his problems very patiently. He then went in front of a pillar and embracing it started shouting, "Help me. The pillar has caught me." Looking at the king, the man started laughing and said, "The pillar has not caught you King, you have caught the pillar. You have to leave the pillar." The king immediately shot back, "This is exactly what you have to realize. Anger has not caught you, you have caught anger – your thoughts

46

invite anger. To get rid of your anger, you have to change your thoughts first." Immediately he took a resolve, "I can get rid of my anger and I shall get rid of it." Subsequently, over a period of time, he was able to replace his old thought patterns with new thoughts and eventually won over his 'anger'.

When the 'I can' and 'I shall' resolve to replace negative habits with thoughts of positive desire get repeatedly bombarded into the conscious mind, messages with new beliefs and feelings start getting fed into the subconscious mind. Eventually, the old programmes in the subconscious mind get replaced by new programmes causing change in attitude.

To condition the attitude, it however is necessary that one frees himself/herself from the 'I consciousness' in a disciplined way. When the 'I consciousness' identifies itself with the undisciplined body-mind complex, human life is dictated by events and circumstances of the world; people become happy with pleasurable events and unhappy with adverse circumstances.

2.9 Impressing the subconscious mind

Whether one acts upon it or not, subconscious mind is working day and night and is always expressing, reproducing, and manifesting according to whatever it is being fed by the conscious mind. Wiliiam James, the father of American psychology, said, "The power to move the world is in your subconscious mind. Your subconscious mind is one with infinite intelligence and boundless wisdom. It is fed by hidden springs.....Whatever you impress upon your subconscious mind; it will move heaven and earth to bring it to pass."

Since subconscious mind expresses involuntarily and effortlessly as an automatic response to external stimuli, it apparently appears to be impossible to control them. However, knowing that the conscious mind processes thoughts, which are the primary trigger for emotions, one can influence the subconscious mind by feeding the desired messages to the conscious mind.

Dale Carnegie rightly said, "If we think happy thoughts, we will be happy. If we think miserable thoughts, we will be miserable. If we think fearful thoughts, we will be fearful. If we think sickly thoughts, we probably will be ill. If we think failure, we will certainly fail. If we wallow in self-pity, everyone will shun us and avoid us."

Processes through which one can influence the subconscious mind are known as 'suggestion', 'self-suggestion' and 'autosuggestion'.

2.10 Suggestion/self & autosuggestion

The objective of suggestion, self-suggestion and autosuggestion is to influence the subconscious mind in order to bring about a change in habit and emotional state by deliberate 'programming' in the subconscious mind.

Suggestion

In simple terms, 'suggestion' is all about impressing an idea or a thought into one's subconscious mind. Therefore, any stimulus sent to the brain through the five senses – seeing, tasting, touching, hearing and smelling is a form of suggestion.

Self-suggestion

Self-suggestion is a process of purposely and deliberately offering stimuli through the five senses. The more one purposely repeats a message with emotion and belief, more effectively it is implanted into his/her subconscious mind.

Autosuggestion

Auto suggestion is a method of communication to subconscious mind through the process of self-suggestion. Its whole idea is to give the subconscious mind repetitive reminder of one's wishes in the form of emotional details and thereby force his/her brain to accept and achieve the reality of his/her own design.

Autosuggestion is practiced through affirmation and visualization

The Wright brothers, Thomas Alva Edison and Alexander Graham Bell had affirmations and visualizations before they had given shape to their dreams and invented aero plane, light bulb and telephone respectively. It is on records that when the result of one of their experiments did not turn out as per their expectation, one of the Wright brothers told his upset brother, "It is all right brother, I can see myself riding in that machine, and it made easily and steadily."

Affirmation is a statement of purpose relevant to certain aspects of one's life that he/she desires to improve. Basically, it is a promise that one makes to himself/herself to strengthen the mind and also to replace negative habits or weak thoughts created by mistaken attitude.

Affirmation involves:

(a)   identification and freezing of what one exactly wants to do or achieve,

(b)   listing and writing down the specific details of everything one can think of doing that will move him/her towards the goal and,

(c)   reviewing the above periodically till strategies are concretized.

Listing intensifies desire and deepens one's belief that the attainment of the objective is possible and writing sends a signal to the subconscious mind that one really wants to accomplish the particular objective. Since thinking precedes writing, it also helps to avoid ambiguity and vagueness.

Affirmation or statement of purposes warrants prioritization of activities and keeping doing something to maintain the momentum.

Visualization is the process or practice of imagining a mental picture of a thing or situation one desires to achieve. It is a technique that uses the human imaginative faculty to make dreams and goals come true.

Being a staunch advocator, Nelson Mandela had written extensively on how visualization had helped him to maintain a positive attitude while he was in prison for twenty seven years. In his autobiography he wrote, "I thought continually of the day when I would walk free. Over and over I fantasized about what I would like to do."

The process of visualization involves:

(a)   repeatedly seeing the objective in the mental picture,

(b)   believing and feeling that one is approaching the goal and the goal is coming nearer and nearer,

(c)   getting the 'feel' of pleasure and happiness that one would have if he/she really achieved the objective.

In autosuggestion, the follow up actions have to be a continuous process over a period of time in line with the suggestion of Swami Vivekananda to follow 'singular idea' which states, "Take up an idea. Make that one idea your life and think of it, dream of it, live on that idea. Let the brain, muscles, nerve and every part of your body be full of that idea and just leave every other idea alone."

If the goals are clearly defined and one is able to make a mental image of the same, one's emotions will steer him/her to make things happen. Napoleon Hill was spot on when he said, "Your ability to use the principle of auto suggestion will depend, very largely, upon your capacity to concentrate upon a given desire until that desire becomes a burning obsession."

Chapter Three

Desire/Motivation/ Goal Setting

Desire originates from thoughts and motivates people to do or achieve 'something'. Strong motivation invariably ends in goal setting. A 'goal' always gives one a direction and enables him/her to measure the progresses/achievements against a task on hand at different stages.

To ensure ease of achievement, a goal can be split into smaller goals. Progressive attainment of smaller goals generates confidence that one is moving in the right direction towards his/her ultimate goal. Multiple goals cause lot of distractions. They are not to be nurtured.

3.1 Dream/Vision - the origin of desire

Dreams play important role in human life. When interviewed by a British press after completing 14,000 runs in test cricket, ace Indian cricketer Sachin Tendulkar said, "Life is flat without dream. I think it is really important to dream and then chase those dreams. It is the dreaming that makes me work so hard." After achieving 100th international centuries in Dhaka on March 2012, he further said (to Rameej Raja, ex. cricket captain of Pakistan), "It is the dreaming and chasing the dreams which keeps me going."

At GoSports Foundation Athletes' Conclave in Bangalore on 17.7.2013, while addressing a vast gathering, Pullela Gopichand the national badminton coach stressing on the power of dreams said, "When I was not playing, I was dreaming of winning all the time. It is important to dream about what we want to become because that effort is as important as anything else." It is rightly said, "Dreams aren't those that you have when you are asleep, dreams are those that don't let you sleep till they are fulfilled."

During his speech while accepting the business man of the year award in 2000, Azim Premji, the Chief of WIPRO said, "........................ One must have strategies to execute dreams, and of course, one must slog to transform dreams into reality. But dreams come first."

History reveals that all big men were dreamers. The Wright brothers dreamt of 'flying', had given shape to their dream, worked hard to ease off all the obstacles that came on their way during experimentation and finally invented aero plane. It is through hard work that dreams become reality.

Human mind does not have the capacity to fabricate stories of its own. Out of more than 50,000 thoughts that pass through the mind of an individual in a day, some are dreams some are visions. Often it is difficult to distinguish between them.

When any thought prominently and frequently plays in the mind, one really wants that to come into existence. It is then given shape and form by the imaginative faculty of the mind. This results in the birth of a 'desire' to achieve or do something.

Desire originates from dream/vision/thought.

3.2 Strong desire leads to motivation

All the achievements and creations in this universe start from deep driving human desires. Upanishads say,

You are what your deep driving desire is;

As your deep driving desire is, so is your will;

As your will is, so is your deed;

As your deed is, so is your destiny.

The prime mover in the success story of any human effort is a 'deep driving desire' from within.

To understand what 'deep driving desire' really means, the following anecdote is very relevant.

Once, the great Greek Philosopher Socrates was asked by a boy, "Sir what is the secret of success?" While explaining, Socrates took the boy to neck deep water and ducked him. The boy was trying to get out of his clutch but Socrates being a strong man repeatedly ducked him. The boy finally was released when he started having breathing problem. After releasing him, Socrates asked the boy, "What did you want most when you were repeatedly ducked in the water?" The boy replied, "Sir, air." Socrates said, "When your desire to achieving 'something' is as intense as when you wanted air, you will achieve success." Desire is the key to motivation. Motivation comes from the word 'motive'. Dictionary meaning of 'motive' is – a factor that influences a person to act in a particular way.

When the desire to achieve an objective comes from within and is very strong, it creates the following two movements:

(a)   a movement from where one is currently placed and

(b)   a movement towards achieving that objective.

The resultant motive for action is called motivation.

3.3   Internal and external motivation

In spite of most of the people being aware what they have to do to make a better life, majority fail to fulfill their desire mainly because either they lack in motivation or their motivation does not last long.

Motivation is classified into two distinct categories – internal motivation and external motivation.

Internal motivation comes from within and is associated with sense of belief, responsibility and pride in accomplishing something. It is self generated and is also called self-motivation. It lasts for a long time. With self-motivation, even the physically handicapped can go beyond the boundaries and perform outstanding activities.

Dr. Shard Kumar Dikshit is a doctor by profession. He was born in Chandrapura in Maharashtra in 1930. After graduating in medical studies from India in 1956, he specialized in plastic surgery from U.S.A and completed further higher studies from London.

While in United States of America, he had a car accident which left his right side paralyzed in 1978. In 1982, he was diagnosed with cancer of the larynx and finally lost his larynx. In 1988, he had a heart attack. In 1994, during his visit to India, he again had a massive heart attack. Immediately, he flew back to U.S.A for triple bypass surgery.

In spite of all these miseries, this partially paralyzed surgeon moving on wheel chair is self-motivated to give poor Indian disfigured patients a new face and a new future free of cost. Though settled in U.S.A, he spends a hectic five months in India every year to take care of his patients. He has special preferences towards the small children and men and women of marriageable age as he does not want them to live with the ignominy of a disfigured face. He says, "Since I am treated as entirely disabled in U.S.A, this is my way of coming back to my country and contributing to life around me. I do cosmic surgery, plastic surgery and correctional surgery that helps the poor, who would not be able to afford it. I see this as my job." This is self-motivation.

When external circumstances create motivation, it is called external motivation. Even though external motivation may lead to quick achievement, it destroys creativity. It does not last for long and works only as long as the motivating factor like incentive, fear etc. persists.

In spite of being the fastest animal on earth, a Cheetah is often outsmarted by its preys during a chase. While Cheetah's motivation is to obtain food, the motivation of the 'prey' is to save its life – a much stronger motivation. This makes the prey surpass nature's law and outsmart the Cheetah during a chase. Motivation of the 'prey' in the above instance is external motivation, it works out of fear.

3.4   Nothing can pacify self-motivation

Self-motivation drives one towards a goal, makes him/her own responsibility, pushes him/her forward when he/she feels like collapsing, shows him/her the light at the end of the tunnel and persuades him/her to remain focused till the goal is achieved. Even setbacks cannot dampen his/her spirit.

Thomas Alva Edison tried 2000 different materials in search of a filament for light bulb. When none worked satisfactorily, one of his assistant complained, "All our work is in vain. We have learned nothing." Edison replied, "Oh! We have come a long way and we have learned a lot. We know that there are two thousand elements we cannot use to make a good light bulb." Even after that he continued to work on the same project and eventually was successful in inventing light bulb which benefitted the entire mankind.

Keroly Takacs was a right handed pistol shooter of Hungary. While representing his country in 1939, an army grenade exploded in his right hand. After that incident, he started practicing shooting left handed and nine years later he won his first gold medal in rapid fire pistol at the London Olympics and won another gold medal at the next Olympic held at Helsinki in 1952 (all with left hand shooting). The above exemplify that nothing can pacify 'self-motivation'.

3.5 Sustained motivation makes winners

To achieve success in any discipline, motivation has to be continuous. It is said, "Most people can stay motivated for two or three months. A few people can stay motivated for two or three years. But a winner can stay motivated for thirty years or as long as it takes to win" – (Anonymous). Sustained motivation pushes people to inculcate in them the ability to drive them harder when the efforts get painful. It makes 'winners'.

History reveals that dreams apparently appearing to be mere impossibility were also realized through sustained motivation.

In 1883, when John Roebling an enthusiastic engineer from U.S.A, conceived the idea to build a bridge between New York and Long Island, he was discouraged outright by all other 'experts' to pursue his concept further. The motivated engineer subsequently started looking for someone to share his views and help him in translating his dream to reality. Finally, he took his son Washington into confidence. Together, the father and the son developed the scheme to accomplish the job. The project finally got started. However, as ill luck would have it, within few months, in a site accident John lost his life and Washington suffered multiple injuries which resulted in his inability to walk, talk or even move. Whole world started criticizing their efforts with mockeries.

One day as he lay on his bed in the hospital, a gentle breeze blew the curtains away and Washington could see the outside world. Instantly, lots of ideas flowed in his mind. He felt he could move one of his fingers. With that finger he tapped his wife's palm. Slowly his wife could decode those tapings into messages and followed the same codes to communicate messages back to her husband. This encouraged Washington. His wife also could figure out that in spite of being handicapped, Washington was not discouraged and still continued to have the burning desire to complete the erection of the bridge. His mind was as sharp as ever. Through his wife he called all his engineers and inspired them to start his unfinished agenda of bridge construction again. For thirteen long years, Washington sent down his instructions and received feedback through his wife's newly developed decoding and coding system. The entire team of engineers remained undaunted by the circumstances and persisted with their efforts and eventually did wonders to complete the project successfully.

Brooklyn Bridge today stands with all the glories as a tribute to the triumph of a man's sustained motivation and indomitable spirit.

3.6   Motivator extracts the best in others

Motivation is a positive spark from within. If someone else tries to light that fire, chances are it will burn very briefly. However, there are people who know how to ignite the potential fire inside others and help them to continue burning. They are known as motivators.

Motivators identify talents with fire within and create conducing atmospheres to ensure that the fire not only burns but also keeps burning. They always challenge, inspire and stimulate people to manifest their full potential. Basically, they act as catalyst and bring about appropriate changes in the thought process of others through recognition, appreciation and inspiration and lead them to aim for higher and higher laurels.

In IISCO, Burnpur, currently known as IISCO Steel Plant, Steel Authority of India Limited, the blast furnace department had a very tough annual production target for the year 1994 - 1995. The then Managing Director of IISCO was very supportive and took lots of personal interest in the performance and development of the blast furnace team. In the month of October, when the team was showing promises of achieving their 'high' monthly target, he asked the blast furnace departmental head to accompany him to participate in a three days workshop organized at Ranchi by Sail's Management training Institute. The workshop was to be chaired by Chairman, SAIL from October 26 to October 28.

On 26th Oct., during dinner hosted for all the delegates, the Managing Director introduced the blast furnace departmental head to the Chairman and said; "He is my trump card. His team is going to achieve the target this month." The Chairman congratulated him for the accelerated production tempo and said, "If your team achieves the target, I shall pay a visit to your plant in Burnpur."

The team achieved the target and Chairman as promised made his visit to Burnpur in the second week of November 1994. During his visit, while interacting with cross section of executives, the Chairman enquired about the blast furnace departmental head. When he stood up, the Chairman said, "Congratulations to your team. I am setting you another target, I am sure your team will achieve it." The team achieved that target too in the month of March, 1995.

Spotting the enthusiasm and realizing the potential of the blast furnace collectives, Chairman Sail and Managing Director, IISCO not only appreciated their efforts but also encouraged and guided them to produce better and better results. They were real motivators.

3.7 Motivation invariably ends in goal setting

Strong motivation invariably ends up in goal setting. About the necessity of goal setting, it is said, "If you don't know where you are going, you are likely to wind up somewhere else." In the game of football, if goal posts are not set in identified positions, all the players will start moving up and down. Similarly in any human effort, if no goals are set, everybody will start drifting and deviating in different directions aimlessly.

Human thoughts and beliefs are creative energies. When directed towards a goal, they get strengthened and give a direction to follow. Goal setting therefore, is not only important, it is a necessity.

Philanthropist Elbert Hubbard says, "Many people fail in life, not for lack of ability or brain or even courage but simply because they never organize their energies around a goal." Walter Staples said, "A goal is a target to shoot at. If we don't have a target to shoot at, how can we score any points? And if we can't score any points, how can we measure any progress? And if we can't measure any progress, how can we get excited about any aspects of our life?"

Goal setting basically is strategic planning. It does not deal with future decisions; it deals with futurity of present decisions.

Goal setting involves looking at where one is at the moment and where he/she wants to be in a given time, and the drafting of appropriate action plans to go there. It is a process of spreading out the sequence of events that have to occur in order that one is able to achieve his/her desired objective.

Goal setting resembles a road map, in which at every point of time, one can know how much he/she has advanced to and how far he/she is away from the destination.

3.8   Considerations involved in goal setting

Walter staple said, "Setting goals and making plans for their accomplishment is one of the master skills in life. Accomplishment is not a function of intelligence, education or specialized training. It comes from holding in mind a clear, precise picture of your heart's desire."

A goal therefore has to be very SPECIFIC.

It has been mentioned in section 3.7, that a goal resembles a road map, in which at every point of time, one can know how much he/she has advanced towards or how far he/she is away from the destination. Knowing where one is, effectively helps him/her to decide his/her need during each subsequent action steps with respect to man, money and other resources.

It implies from above that a goal has to be MEASURABLE.

With careful planning, one can often foresee if at some point he/she is likely to face a problem. This enables him/her to make contingency plans if necessary. It is easier to prepare for an anticipated crisis rather than to deal with it when it surfaces unexpected. Efficient thinkers always assume that the worst will happen and make provisions against them. Napoleon Bonaparte was once asked if he believed in luck. He replied, "Yes, I do. I believe in bad luck. I believe I will always have it, and I plan accordingly."

While explaining the basics of goal setting, Canadian Paralympian Rick Hansen, the final torch lighter in 2010 Winter Olympic said, "It should be challenging enough to make you stretch but not so far that you break." The above means that a goal –

(a)   has to be beyond one's grasp but within his/her reach. It has to be ACHIEVABLE.

(b)   should be high enough to motivate yet REALISTIC enough to avoid discouragement.

Goals are dreams with deadlines. Once one sets a goal for any activities in life, fixing a time frame is mandatory. Planning to achieve a goal without time frame is meaningless.

A goal therefore has to be TIME SPECIFIC.

Setting a goal and planning to achieve it should always be put in writing. Since thinking precedes writing, it helps to avoid ambiguity and vagueness. Albert Einstein very succinctly said, "A goal properly set is half reached."

3.9   Splitting of goal is always beneficial

A mountaineer does not climb the peak only by thinking or doing it in one large step. He/she starts at the bottom and slowly makes his/her way to the top step by step. In any walk of life, achieving a goal becomes simpler when it is split into smaller goals.

Progressive attainment of smaller goals in predetermined sequences within identified time frames gives one the confidence that he/she is approaching the goal in the right direction and generates belief that the ultimate goal can also be achieved successfully.

Each time one reaches a milestone along the path to the ultimate destination, especially when the journey is long, it boosts his/her confidence and his/her commitment towards the task. Henry Ford said, "Nothing is particularly hard, if you divide it into small jobs."

Sir Donald Bradman of Australia was one of the all time great cricketers of the world. When he retired from test cricket, journalists surrounding him asked, "Your batting average for the career stands at fabulous 99.96 %. What was your philosophy and what motivated and inspired you to achieve such a high level of performance?" Bradman candidly replied, "Every time I went to bat, right up to the moment I faced the first ball, I used to think and concentrate on not getting out in the first ball. Surviving the first ball faced, I used to concentrate on scoring a run. After scoring a run, I used to concentrate on a target of 10....20....40....100....200....300....400....." Twice in his career, he scored more than 400 runs in first class cricket.

Bradman paced all his cricketing innings setting targets in steps. On reaching one milestone, he always set his eyes in the next level. The above philosophy of Bradman is a demonstration that there is no way under the sun that one will ever achieve the highest goal unless he/she has fulfilled the lesser ones.

3.10 Multiple goals create distractions

During the music launch of a film in Mumbai (Telegraph, Kolkata, and 23rd Jan 2013) Cricketer Sachin Tendulkar was asked if he has any plan to make a silver screen debut. He said, "Till the time I am playing cricket, it will only be cricket. I will do one thing at a time." It is relevant to quote Plato in this context. He said, "Each man is capable of doing one thing well. If he attempts several, he will fail to achieve distinction in any."

Saurav Ganguly the famous skipper of Indian cricket team, conducted the television show 'Dadagiri' part one as an anchor in Zee Bangla. In one of the episodes, in reply to some of the questions asked by the parents of the participating little kids, he said that in his early school days even though he was proficient in football and studies, towards the later part when he realized that if he concentrated on all the disciplines, he would not be able to excel in any, he decided to fully concentrate on cricket. Football was pushed to the back seat and studies were also compromised to quite an extent so that he could get more time and energy to devote on cricket. Thereafter, he was thoroughly involved in continually improving his cricketing skills. He did not allow any distraction to make dent on his focus and concentration.

It was his single minded devotion and concentration towards a singular goal that eventually enabled him to become a very successful cricketer of international repute.

Singular goal creates a purpose that often does not get distracted. The importance of singular goal has been aptly summed up in a Chinese proverb. It says, "If you chase two rabbits, both will escape." It means that if one puts all his efforts and energies into trying to fulfill two goals at the same time, he/she will not succeed in either. With multiple goals things often get foggy from one's perspective because of more of distractions; it then becomes very difficult to concentrate and remain focused on any objective on sustained basis.

Chapter Four

Nothing Happens of Its Own

Nothing happens of its own. Even good thoughts and talent cannot guarantee success; they need to be complemented by focus towards and passion for the task on hand, uninterrupted hard work, perseverance and utilization of the present without worrying about the past and the future.

4.1 Brushing off thoughts of limitations

Even though mankind has numbers of limitations with respect to other creatures, nature has blessed the mankind with many advantages like,

(a) ability to think, analyze and rethink again and again if necessary,

(b) intelligence and capability to create their own environments, and

(c) stretchable hard working capacity.

It is said that if one takes out the DNA that creates the programme for human body, it will reveal that even a fraction of the brain is more dynamic and complex than NASA's rocket launching station. Talking about enormous human potential, Thomas Alva Edison said, "If we all did the things we are capable of doing, we would literally astound ourselves."

In spite of holding in reserve unlimited powers within as explained above, all human 'potential' however do not blossom into fulfillment. The reasons can be attributed to

(a) ignorance and   (b) thoughts of limitations.

(a) *Ignorance:* Most of the people are ignorant about their capabilities as a result they fail to utilize them. This is corroborated by inspirational writer Norman Vincent Peale's observation. He said, "Most of the individuals do not have adequate conception of the inherent powers and abilities they possess."

(b) ***Thoughts of limitations:*** Thought of limitation saps the energy within and weakens the mind.

Though history reveals that there is no constraint in human mind, no walls around human spirit and no barrier to progress, in reality, many people do carry pre-conceived notions which wittingly or unwittingly impose limitations on their own capabilities.

Study on the bumblebee by the scientists reveal that its body is too heavy, wing span small and aerodynamically it cannot fly. Being unaware of the above, the bumblebee keeps on flying. Like bumblebee, if one remains free and open minded and thinks, plans and puts in hard work, he/she can utilize his/her full potential and do great things in life. Human mind like parachute works best when it is open.

Brushing off thoughts of limitation therefore, is very important and essential. Robert collier rightly advocated, "...you must think abundance, see abundance, feel abundance, believe abundance...... Let no thought of limitation enter your mind."

I remember the Inter College Cricket Championship final in 1968-69 when I was in the fourth year of my engineering course. Our team had a very strong batting lineup. However, in that particular match, batting first, we were all out for a paltry 120 odd runs. The opposition team was 21 for no loss at the first drinks break. At that stage, all of us practically accepted defeat mentally. The vice captain of our team however felt differently. Seeing the demoralizing body language and the drooping shoulders of the players, he quickly remarked, "How does it matter how much we have scored? What matters is we have to get the opposition all out below our score. The game is wide open; it is still possible for us to win." These words had electrifying effect on the players. When play resumed, the body language of the entire team was totally changed. There appeared to be purposes behind each of their moves in the field. The result was an unbelievable victory for us. The opposition was bundled out for 36 runs.

Human life is a replica of the game of cricket – where nothing is impossible. In fact, possibility and impossibility start in the mind first. Thoughts of limitations therefore, should never be allowed to make their home in the mind.

4.2   Things have to be made to happen

Many people wish but eventually, fail to achieve their goal mainly because they either do hard work without proper thinking, or think deeply without doing the necessary hard work. Some even idle away their time doing neither. There are also others who lack the tenacity to keep their focus on a chosen path for a prolonged period. However, seeing others achieve success, especially in the discipline in which they wish to excel, all these people start comparing themselves with others and attribute 'others' success to luck. This is a hardcore reality in life.

I remember accompanying a reputed national table tennis player to watch a table tennis test match between India and Japan in Kolkata in the early seventies. When I saw Manjit Dua turning out for India, my memory of contesting him in equal terms during the combined North and East Zone Inter University Table Tennis meet held at IIT, Kanpur in 1969, flashed in my memory. I could not believe that in the interim period, he could improve his game to the level of qualifying to represent India, when I did not even figure in the selection of the state team. So, I made an adverse comment about his selection in the Indian team. When my companion who was an outstanding player in the zonal and national level promptly reminded me that Manjit Dua was an automatic choice for the Indian team based on his consistent performance in the national championships for the past two years, reality dawned on me.

I realized that,

(a) Manjit Dua had made things happen,

(b) simply measuring abilities against others at a particular stage in life means nothing.

In my career as a steel plant professional, I have seen many successful professionals from close quarters. They started at par with others but subsequently raised their level of performance so high that they left others far behind in the long run. Persistent efforts to convert thoughts to reality made them successful in their journey forward while others stagnated or even got reduced to insignificance.

Talent alone cannot make things happen. They need to be supported by

(a) clear thinking of what one wants to achieve,

(b) passion for the task on hand and focused attention towards it,

(c) uninterrupted hard work,

(d) perseverance with never say quit resolve,

(e) utilization of present without worrying about the past or the future,

(f) commitment and courage to take decisions in time.

Wise people rightly say that one has to think things through and then follow through with actions till his/her objectives are achieved. Nothing will happen of its own. John F. Kennedy was spot on when he said, "Things do not happen. Things are made to happen."

4.3 Focused attention becomes powerful

The sun is a powerful source of energy and is soaking the earth with billions of kilowatts of energy every hour. Even then with minimum protections, one can survive its scorching effects. However, a laser, with much less energy when focused in a coherent stream of light, drills a hole in diamond. Alexander Graham Bell said, "Concentrate all your thoughts upon the work on hand. The sun's rays do not burn until brought to focus." Sunlight falling directly on palm does not cause burn, but when it is focused on the palm through magnifying glass, it does. Similarly, when human attention is focused towards an objective, it becomes a very powerful tool.

Focusing can be explained as a process of diverting scattered attentions into a chosen track and follow it up till the objectives are achieved. It is a discipline which most people find hard to maintain for any length of time, yet it is essential in the journey of life. It is the way forward towards achieving excellence.

Focused attention:

(a) harnesses energy towards a desired goal,

(b) gives ideas 'time to develop',

(c) brings clarity to all the action plans involved while approaching a goal,

(d) pushes one for periodical review of progress and,

(e) helps in maintaining concentration and enthusiasm for a long stretch of time.

Without focus, one's

(a) effort becomes half hearted,

(b) attention span gets shortened,

(c) concentration becomes ineffective and,

(d) enthusiasm diminishes.

In the sixties, four months after Kennedy took charge as the President of U.S.A and moved to the white house, he made that historic speech announcing America's plan of sending a man to moon within a stipulated time frame. People were taken aback. Christopher Klaft, a NASA Engineer and later Chief Director of

Apollo Flights sarcastically remarked, "I thought that he had lost his mind. We had only fifteen minutes of flights under our belt in space, we had not yet succeeded in setting a mercury capsule into orbit, and here comes a guy who tells me we are going to the moon." Eventually, America did achieve the feat and that too within the dead line set by Kennedy.

Kennedy's 'announcement' put the focus of the entire team on a track and pushed them to plan meticulously and follow through with precision and achieve the goal exactly 164 days before the target date announced by Kennedy.

4.4 Passion smoothen follow through

The secret of life is not in doing what one likes, but in liking what he/she does. When one does not like what he/she does, he/she does not do it with much conviction, optimism and enthusiasm. Even an easy task becomes difficult when it is done with reluctance. When one likes what he does, he/she is said to have developed a passion for the task on hand.

It is rightly said that,

(a)   without passion, a person is merely a latent force and a possibility only,

(b)   even God likes to know again and again what one likes to have. It is not that He forgets one's dreams and prayers, but He loves to check his/her passion towards his/her task on hand.

Passion makes one intensely enthusiastic while carrying out a task. Nothing needs to motivate him/her and all his/her follow through actions become very smooth and natural. He/she does not even feel the ordeal of hard work.

Thomas Alva Edison who was passionate about whatever he did in his life, corroborated the above statement. He said, "I never did a day's work in my life. It was all fun."

Thomas Alva Edison had passion for scientific experimentation on innovative ideas. During his early teens, he used to sell newspapers named 'Detroit Free Press' while travelling in the train between Detroit and Port Huron. Since he had plenty of free time after selling off the newspapers, he utilized the time by conducting various experiments in a small laboratory set up by him in the luggage van. Arising out of ignition of some of the chemicals, one day fire broke out in the van. The guard immediately stopped the train, slapped Edison in the ear and forced him to get down along with all his belongings. After that incident, even though he became partially deaf, his passion for innovative experimentation did not take any beating. It was so intense that he again started from the scratch and continued with his 'experimentations' and made many inventions for the benefit of mankind.

Passion is a driving force. Albert Einstein very succinctly said, "I have no special talent, I am only passionately curious."

4.5 Hard work with application of mind

It is said, "Hard work beats talent when talent does not work hard." Hard work devoid of any purpose is often painful and frustrating; however, when one has a strong purpose, it becomes a necessity. This is how Napoleon described his philosophy of life while talking about hard work, "I think a great deal........................ ..... There exists no guardian angel who suddenly and mysteriously whispers in my ear what I have to do or say. Everything is turned over in my mind, again and again, whether I am at table or at the theatre. At night, I wake up in order to work."

The daily grind of hard work makes one polished and pushes him/her to be better prepared to extract the maximum out of any given situation and helps in the –

(a)   realization of self-potential and

(b)   development and enhancement of his/her capabilities further.

After finishing a concert, the great violinist Fritz Kreisler was once told by an observer, "I would give my life to play the way you do." Kreisler replied in a cool voice, "I exactly did that."

Great musician Paderewski spent long hours on practice to hone his music. After a concert, one of his fans once asked him the secret of his success. He replied, "Practice. If I don't practice for a day I can feel the difference. If I don't practice for two days, my critics discover. And if I don't practice for three days, the whole world comes to know." It is rightly said that one has to fall in love with hard work and put in many small efforts which others cannot see or appreciate before he/she achieves anything worthwhile. Painter Michelangelo, once said, "If people knew how hard I had to work to gain my mastery, it would not seem wonderful at all."

Hard work however must not be construed as physical efforts only. Along with hard work, applying the mind and knowing where to put in the effort is equally important.

A forest officer once recruited few employees. In the first week, the performance of one of the employee was outstanding. On an average, he cut 20 trees per day against others average of 12 trees per day. From the second week onwards his efficiency started progressively getting down and at the end of the fourth week his average daily cutting rate came down to 12 trees per day. Being disturbed, the forest officer called the employee and asked him, "When did you sharpen your axe last?" The employee replied, "The day before I was interviewed by you for the job." The officer said, "Immediately sharpen your axe. For efficient cutting, the axe needs periodical sharpening." The performance of the employee improved again after that.

4.6 Results always follow efforts put in

In any human endeavour, to get results one has to put in effort first. When a stone cutter attempts to split a stone, he goes on hammering even though no signs of crack appear on the surface. Finally when it splits, say on 101 blows, the stone cutter understands and realizes that the 'splitting' is caused by the cumulative effect of 101 hammerings not the 101th hammering in isolation.

While putting in efforts, the mind has to be filled with feelings of victory. If the feelings of failure creep in the mind, it will kill the efforts, neutralize the 'purpose' and make success impossible.

Scientist C.V. Raman tirelessly toiled with absolute focus on his projects throughout his life. When he was posted in Kolkata on a Government job in the Financial Civil Service, it is said that off duty he used to devote time in conducting his research work in the laboratories of Association of Cultivation of Science. His working schedule during that period as recorded by one of his associates was as follows.

(a) Between 5:30 a.m. and 9:45 a.m., he spent time in the laboratory of The Cultivation of Science. After reaching home, he used to quickly gulp food and immediately rush for his office invariably by a taxi to be on time for work.

(b) Between 5:30 p.m. and 9:30 p.m., on his way back from the office, he again spent time in the laboratory. Sundays were spent entirely at the laboratory.

Eventually, he resigned from the lucrative Government job to take up professorship of University College of Science, Kolkata. Even after becoming a Professor, he used to work at the laboratory for long hours. While at work, many times he used to fall asleep in the table itself (out of exhaustion) till he was awakened next morning by his assistants.

While working on the discovery of 'Raman effect', he once told his assistant Dr. K. S. Krishnan, "We must pursue it and we are on the right lines...............The Nobel Prize must be won." His efforts, confidence and tenacity ultimately won him the Nobel Prize.

Nothing comes easy in life, one has to work for everything, and the result is often commensurate with the amount of work one puts in.

4.7 Perseverance is an essential tool

A flowing river makes its way through rocks not because of its power, but because of its persistence. Many people have great goals and visions. However, when the desired results do not materialize as quickly or as easily as they anticipate, they lose interest, give up and never try again. They simply lack in perseverance. To move forward in any discipline of life, perseverance is an essential tool. History reveals that all great performers achieved their success by staying afloat in their efforts with patience in abundance. Dale Carnegie said, "Most of the important things in this world have been accomplished by people who have kept on trying when there seemed to be no hope at all."

Perseverance is defined as sustained belief or effort in spite of obstacles, difficulties or discouragement. It has tremendous positive power. Albert Einstein often said, "Finish whatever you start. It is not that I am smart; it is just that I stay with the problem longer."

The following sequence of events took place in the life of Abraham Lincoln. He struggled relentlessly throughout his career without losing his spirit and enthusiasm and ultimately became a very successful President of America. He was an example of spirited thoughts, hard work and perseverance under all circumstances.

– Born in 1809, in a poor farmer family. He had no formal schooling.

– At 21, he lost job as store keeper because of owner's bankruptcy.

- At 24, borrowed money for business and became broke by year end.
- The above loan had to be paid in 17 years.
- At 26, engaged to be married, but his sweetheart died.
- At 27, had nervous breakdown. It needed six month's bed rest.
- At 40, applied for but did not get land officer's job.
- At 45, lost senatorial race.
- At 45, earned license to practice law (through self-learning).
- At 45, lost to become vice-president.
- At 49, lost senatorial race.
- At 51, became President of U.S.A in 1860.

The above reminds the observation of the great Chinese philosopher Confucius. He said, "Our greatest glory is not in never falling but in rising every time we fall." The famous French chemist and biologist Louis Pasteur openly declared that the strength and secret of his success was - "tenacity."

4.8 'Quitting' ensures permanent defeat

Failure is temporary but quitting makes it permanent. Human life is similar to the game of boxing where defeat is not declared when one is in pain or he/she falls; it is declared when he/she fails to 'get up' to continue fighting. Quitting guarantees defeat.

As an inventor, Thomas Alva Edison made thousands of unsuccessful attempts at inventing the light bulb. But, he never gave up and eventually invented light bulb which blessed the life of entire mankind. When a reporter asked him how he felt on being unsuccessful in thousand attempts, he replied, "I did not fail thousand times. The light bulb was an invention with thousands of steps."

Failure is not the worst thing that can happen to an individual, but the fear of failure is. Fear of failure basically is a future projection of worry and reliance on what happened in the past. It is the fear of failure which often prompts one to quit when the going gets tough.

Fear has different meaning to different people. To some it means 'Forget everything and run' (Quit) while to others it means 'Face everything and rise'. Those who follow the second option, achieve success.

While learning to walk, infants keep on falling but they get up and try to walk again. If they stop getting up, they will never learn walking.

It is said that after repeatedly failing to achieve whatever he wanted to (refer section 4.7), in around 1958, Abraham Lincoln felt so much frustrated that he wrote to one of his close friends, "I am now the most miserable man living. If what I feel were equally distributed to the whole human family, there would not be a single cheerful face on the earth." He however did not quit. His optimism and enthusiasm uplifted his sagging spirit. Eventually, he went on to become the president of America within next two years.

4.9 Utilization of the 'present' is important

Mike Atherton, ex. England cricket captain and sports journalist quoted ace cricketer Sachin Tendulkar as saying, "The mind always tries to be in the past or future. It never wants to be in the present. My batting is at its best when my mind is in present. It does not happen naturally. You have to take yourself there"(The Telegraph, July 22, 2011, Kolkata). Paddy Upton, the mental conditioning coach of World Cup winning Indian cricket team in 2011, while talking about Sachin Tendulkar's longevity in International cricket said, "Sachin does not buy into the expectations...He stays in the present and, by doing so, there's is no anxiety over what may happen in the future. It is the now for him" (The Telegraph, May 25, 2013, Kolkata).

Making full use of the present is of prime importance. It is a gift of God to the mankind. Famous musician Babatunde Olatunji candidly says,

Yesterday is history, tomorrow is a mystery.

And today? Today is a gift

That is why we call it the present.

Swami Vivekananda said, "If what we are now has been the result of our past actions, it certainly follows that whatever we wish to be in future can be produced by our present actions."

The present holds the grave of the past and the seed of the future. In the words of Einstein, the only way to properly address the future is to be as present as possible in the 'present'.

Living in the present ensures peace and cheerfulness of mind. Lord Buddha was once sitting in a gathering surrounded by his disciples. The face of all the disciples reflected peace and cheerfulness. A prince sitting nearby looked sad and gloomy. Noting the difference, a learned visitor asked Buddha, "Sir, why in spite of their hard lives, your disciples are all full of peace and delight, while the prince to whom all the luxuries and comforts are available, looks sad and without cheer?" Buddha replied, '...... They do not brood over the past or worry over the future. They always live in the present and move with the present. This is the secret of their peace and cheerfulness."

4.10 Worry causes loss of time & energy

Dale Carnegie said, "If you can't sleep, then get up and do something instead of lying there worrying. It is the worry that gets you not the lack of sleep."

Worry is a complete cycle of inefficient thought around either past or future. It works slowly but persistently till one's reasoning faculty is disturbed and his/her confidence takes a beating.

Worry never rids tomorrow of its sorrows, but hinders today's joys. Past is already gone and the future is yet to come. One has no control on either of these. If one worries too much, it will eat into his/her 'present'. It is rightly said, "You can neither change the past nor you can plan the future, but you can ruin the present by worrying about them."

Worry is a state of mind which always gives a small thing a big shadow. It is a misuse of imagination.

Sir Winston Churchill once said, "When I look back on all these worries, I remember the story of the old man who said on his death bed that he had had a lot of troubles in his life most of which never happened."

A woman had a tendency to get worried over even small issues. She was once asked by one of her friends to keep a diamond bracelet for few days when she planned an outstation trip. To ensure double safety, the woman immediately went to a jeweler's shop to purchase a strong casket to keep the bracelet. Seeing the bracelet the jeweler told the lady, "The diamonds of the bracelets are artificial. So, you need not worry about purchasing any casket." Hearing this, the lady heaved a sigh of relief and said, "Thank God, my worries are over."

It implies from above that worry often is created by attaching unnecessary importance to anticipated problem which may not even exist/occur in reality. Like people they grow, if nurtured.

Chapter Five

Learning Ensures Growth

Learning, unlearning and relearning are essential for confidence building which ultimately ensures growth. Everybody gets opportunity to learn from different situations in life. Those opportunities need to be properly made use of. No learning ever goes into waste.

Periodical self-assessment and expecting as well as accepting change as the way of life helps one to prepare better and move in the right direction in life. Self-pity is a progress breaker and needs to be shunned.

5.1 Necessity of learning/unlearning/relearning

Albert Einstein was spot on when he said, "I do not think much of a man who is not wiser today than he was yesterday." The purpose of learning is growth.

An extract from the speech delivered by Mr. Narayan Murty (Chairman and CEO of Infosys Technologies Limited) while accepting the award for the 'Businessman of the year in 1999, is very relevant in this context. He said, "As we move forward, there is a lot that Infosys has to learn from every corporation in the country. However, I will mention just a few. We have to learn from the –

(a)   longevity of Hindustan Lever,

(b)   compassion of the Tatas,

(c)   patriotism of the Bajajs,

(d)   quality standards of TVS,

(e)   dynamism of the Ambanis and

(f)   customer friendliness of HDFC."

Learning is a continuous process. Learning in general is not difficult, but learning to ever keep learning is. A kid picks up a new language quite easily and in a natural way. But while learning a second language, he/she often makes use of the first language which proves to be a handicap. The new learning becomes easier the moment he/she lets the knowledge of the first language go. 'Unlearning' therefore, is a prerequisite for one to learn something new. Unlearning is the process by which one eliminates old logic and behaviour to make room for new ones. Knowledge grows, and simultaneously becomes obsolete as the reality changes. Understanding the above therefore involves

(a)   acquiring knowledge,

(b)   unlearning the obsolete and

(c)   relearning (i.e. adding) new knowledge.

Sarah Caldwell, founder of Boston Opera group, currently known as Opera Company of Boston said, "Learn everything you can, anytime you can and from anyone you can. There will always come a time when you will be grateful that you did." There are lots one can learn even from the mistakes made by others. Chanakya once said, "Learn from the mistakes of others. You can't live long enough to make them all yourself." Learning never goes into waste.

Self-assessment is essential for development

For development, self-assessment is an absolute necessity. Monitoring, evaluating and assessing self on regular basis help in the identification of areas where improvements are to be brought about. It also helps one to acquire new knowledge. Individuals can adapt different methods for self-assessment. A typical example is mentioned underneath.

One day a little boy went to a telephone booth which was in the cash counter of a store. As the boy dialed a number and started talking, the owner of the store was observing the boy and listening to the conversation. The boy was talking to a lady. Their conversation went as follows:

Boy: Lady, can you give me the job of cutting your lawn?

Lady: I already have someone to cut my lawn.

Boy: Lady, I will cut your lawn for half the price than the person who cuts your lawn.

Lady: I am very satisfied with the person who is presently cutting my lawn.

Boy: Lady, I'll even sweep the floor and stairs of your house for free.

Lady: No, thank you.

With a smile on his face, the boy put back the receiver on the telephone. The store owner, who was listening to the conversation walked up to talk to the boy. Following is the excerpts of the interaction between them.

Store owner: Son! I like your attitude. I liked the positive spirit and would like to offer you a job.

Boy: No, thank you, Sir.

Store owner: But few minutes back you were really pleading for a job?

Boy: Sir, I was just checking my performance at the job I already have. I am the one who is working for the lady I was talking to.

5.2 Ignorance is not shameful, unwilling to learn is

It is said that people are constantly given lessons in life. If one does not learn the lessons, he/she is tested again with the lessons repeated in another shape or form. The lessons often start easy and become harder the second time around.

Whether one likes it or not or calls it natural unfolding of events, the above phenomenon is happening and will continue to occur as long as one is breathing.

I remember my training days in Indian Iron and Steel Company, Burnpur in 1971. We had been put through a plant orientation programme in which we had to spend a fortnight in each of the departments followed by an interview to assess our learning. We had been instructed to keenly observe the details of functioning of each department and record them in a diary. Since training was given in groups, many of us including me gave diary maintenance a miss.

While interviewed by the power department chief, I landed up in trouble. We were individually asked to show him the diary from where he was asking questions. When my turn came, I snatched the diary of one of my colleagues, tore off the first page bearing his name and entered the interview room. My performance was miserable. I could not explain many of the observations recorded in that diary. Obviously, I was asked to prepare for a repeat interview.

During dinner at night, when we batch mates were discussing about the 'interview', our seniors impressed upon us the seriousness of these interviews and cautioned us saying that in the previous year a trainee was sacked for poor performance. I became panicky and started maintaining a technical diary from the next day itself which I still maintain.

Though I initially ignored diary maintenance, the fear of losing job forced me to develop the habit. Every individual gets signal to learn, correct and update himself/herself. If the signals are ignored, he/she is brought to life with a sledge hammer.

Exposures are opportunities for self upliftment. As a steel plant professional, I had the experience of being exposed to various departments in different periods. On quite a number of occasions, I cut a sorry figure while representing the current department in discussions. This however never discouraged me as every time I came out of such discussions, I got enriched in knowledge at least on few counts. Exposure to any new environment always gives one an opportunity to learn and upgrade his/her knowledge. It is relevant in this context to refer to the following anecdote.

Thomas Alva Edison was once invited by a school to encourage and inspire the students. During interactions, one of the students asked him, "Sir, how could you acquire so much of knowledge?"

He promptly replied, "By telling others that I don't know, but that I was very keen to learn."

Wise people rightly say, "Being ignorant is not shameful, but being unwilling to learn is."

5.3 Scope for learning exists even in criticism

Only the doers are criticized. This is a hardcore reality in life. Dale Carnegie rightly said, "Nobody kicks a dead dog." Criticism is a part of life. The more one is accomplished in life, the more he/ she risks of being criticized. As the success rate increase, numbers of critics also multiply and they start becoming louder.

Many times one unwittingly fails to notice certain defects which are brought to light through criticism. Criticisms basically act as a mirror which enables one to see the dirt (if any) on the face which otherwise cannot be seen. Inability to cope with criticism is a sign of poor self esteem.

Criticism which initially appears to be hard to digest but in the long run turns out to be gentle rain that nourishes growth without destroying the roots, is known as 'just' or 'constructive' criticism. If properly listened to and understood in broader perspective, 'Just' or 'Constructive' criticism always benefit people in the long run. Swami Vivekananda always advocated, "I love those who criticize me, as they are my teachers in my path of self-growth."

Criticism arising out of ignorance or jealousy is known as 'unjust' criticism.

Once when Lord Buddha was in meditation, a man went close to him and started abusing, "You have no right to teach others. You are as stupid as anyone else. You are a fake." The man finally cooled down after exhausting all his abuses. When Lord Buddha got up from his meditation, he asked the man, "If someone gives you something and you don't take, then with whom does that thing remain?" The man replied, "Obviously, that will remain with the giver." Buddha smiled and replied, "In that case, I do not accept the abuses you had given me." The man realized his folly. The above is unjust criticism arising out of ignorance and Lord Buddha just brushed it off.

In my steel plant career, I had experience with some of the people who initially took interest in helping others. However, when 'others' started taking care of themselves, they became critical and tried to destabilize 'others', made 'others' feel uncomfortable and sometimes even went to the extent of making their life miserable. Basically, such things happen out of jealousy. In professional as well as personal life, these are common happenings. One has to be aware of this and not get disheartened when faced with such situations. Best way to deal with criticisms out of jealousy is to take them as a silent compliment.

One should always take the positives out of criticisms and brush off the rest and ensure that criticism does not make any dent in his/her confidence level. The following quote from W. Clement Stone is very relevant in the above context, "Don't mind criticism. If it is untrue, disregard it. If it is unfair, keep from irritations. If it is ignorant, smile. If it is justified, learn from it."

5.4 To grow, adapting to changes is necessary

It is said that it is neither the strongest nor the most intelligent, but the one most responsive to change who ultimately survives. Adapting to change is necessary for growth. The world is moving fast and lot of changes are taking place. What is true today may not be true tomorrow. What works today may not work tomorrow. One has to keep pace with the changes, otherwise he/she will be swept away and finally perish into insignificance.

Change has varied psychological impact on human mind. To the

(a)   fearful, it is threatening because they think that with changes things might get worse.

(b)   hopeful, it is encouraging because they think that with changes things will get better.

(c)   confident, it is inspiring because they think that by adapting to change they can create situations of their own liking and desire.

People in general, develop a tendency to resist change because they overestimate the value of what they have and underestimate the value of what they may gain by giving it up. It is not that some people have will power and some don't. The reality is, some people are ready to change and the others are not. The latter change only when the pain of what they go through becomes greater than the fear of change.

It is said, "When you want to change your circumstances, you must first change your thinking." To be compatible with the changing environment, one has to be ready to shift his/her focus from what he/she is to what he/she might become and be very clear in his/her thinking. When one changes the way he/she looks at things, the things he/she looks at also change. Winston Churchill said, "To improve is to change. To be perfect is to change often."

5.5   Changes do not take place overnight

If a frozen block of ice at below zero degrees centigrade is heated, for some time no change will apparently be visible. But when a temperature of zero degree is attained, ice block starts melting and gradually gets converted to water. If the heating is continued further, at around hundred degrees centigrade the water starts boiling and ultimately gets converted to steam. The change of ice to water and water to steam does not take place instantly after heating starts. In human life too, changes take place over a period of time. One therefore, should never hold the belief that by adapting to change, everything in his/her life will miraculously start happening overnight.

Unlike an 'event' that yields instant result, a 'change' is a process which works over a period of time.

After the sudden death of his father, Azim Premji took charge of WIPRO (Western India Vegetable Products) when he was still a student abroad (in 1966). Assessing the market scenario and sensing a change, he set his mind in the diversification of company's products. His farsightedness to anticipate and adapt to prospective changing business scenario eventually paid dividends in later years. It elevated WIPRO to the level of a big conglomerate with a turnover of Rs 2,000 crores in 2000 from the level of a Rs 4 crores turnover edible oil company in 1966. WIPRO currently is a name to be reckoned with in the field of Information technology in the world.

5.6 Confidence always inspires and drives

Confidence is an expression of feelings of being secured in ability, decision making and actions. It makes one stronger and more relaxed internally and always puts him/her in the right frame of mind to go after problem solving. Confidence need not be inherited; it can be acquired. Dale Carnegie said, "Action breeds confidence and courage." Facing and overcoming of difficult situation gives one the confidence that since he/she has lived through it, he/she can face whatever situation comes in his/her way in future.

Hard work is one of the most essential key to confidence building. Bruce Lee developed so much of confidence through long hours of hard work that he often said, "To hell with circumstances. I create my opportunity."

Confident people are not bothered about how others view their efforts at different stages. During his heydays Mohammad Ali the famous boxer, would often say, "It is a job. Grass grows, birds fly, waves pound the sand, I beat people up." He exactly did that in reality.

Irrespective of circumstances, confidence inspires one to

(a)   make the best of what he/she has,

(b)   seize opportunities where others see only problems,

(c)   bounce back even from disastrous situations.

Confident people are always open to learning. Overconfidence however leads to arrogance and hinders learning.

5.7   Concentration on strength is important

Who does not have weaknesses? Many people however are obsessed with their weaknesses to such an extent that they develop a tendency to focus and concentrate more on the weak links and underutilize their strengths in the process. Of course, it is necessary to be aware of the weaknesses so that corrective measures can be implemented in time; however history reveals that success had always been achieved by those who concentrated and used their strengths the most instead of looking for extraneous help.

Swami Vivekananda said, "The remedy for weakness is not brooding over weakness, but thinking of strength."

In April 2001, all the three running blast furnaces (B.F 2, B.F 3 and B.F 4) in IISCO, Burnpur were limping and the plant financially was not in a position to immediately organize capital repair of any of these furnaces. Under the prevailing circumstances, immediate and quick revival of no. 1 blast furnace at low cost appeared to be the only viable option for the survival of the steel plant. The task however was very difficult as this furnace was shut down abruptly in 1998, without any burden preparation.

G.M (Iron and Steel) in consultation with the senior executives (to be referred as 'think tank') decided to revive the furnace without any major dismantling of equipment and refractory. Anticipated jobs were listed and broken down to different packages and different groups were formed to carry out the jobs package wise.

During the first meeting of the 'think tank' with the group in-charges to freeze the repair schedule, the 'group in-charges' came out with the following observations:

(a) No. 1 blast furnace was put down in 1998, without proper 'burden preparation' and proper 'blowing down'.

(b) The furnace before the shut down had numbers of maintenance problems which needed attention.

(c) Many of the equipments and facilities of no. 1 blast furnace were already utilized as spares in the other 500 cu. m blast furnace (no. 2 Blast furnace) operating in the plant at that moment.

Citing above, they expressed that a low budget, short and quick repair did not appear to be feasible. The 'think tank' however convinced the group in-charges to keep the need of the company as the topmost priority of the hour. They were asked to analyze the situation further with more emphasis on their strength and think, act and rise beyond their past experiences of similar repairs.

During the second meeting with the groups after 48 hours, the 'think tank'

(a) expressed their confidence on the capabilities of the groups,

(b) assured full support to the groups at every stage and,

(c) announced 30th June as the lighting up date of the furnace after necessary repair.

All the group in charges were then asked to back track and work out their repair schedules matching with the final lighting up date and identify their requirements of men, material and money. This time, the group in charges responded in affirmative, worked out the micro details of all the activities after fine tuning the action plans. This enabled the think tank to quickly finalize the action points and obtain administrative and financial approval from the competent authority. To the delight of everybody, the jobs were carried out as per the plan and the furnace was lighted up on 30th June 2001.

The collectives utilized their full strengths and did what could be done and ensured that what could not be done did not interfere with what could be done. In the process, against all odds they completed the task which in the initial stage appeared to be 'impossible'.

5.8   Life simply is reflection of human actions

A son and his father were walking on a mountain. The son suddenly fell, got hurt and screamed, "Ouch!" He was surprised to hear the same utterance after a time gap. Being curious to know the source of the voice, he yelled, "Who are you?" He received the answer: "Who are you?" Angered at the response, he again screamed, "Who are you?" And received the same answer: "Who are you?"

Confused, the son wanted to know from the father what was happening. Explaining, the father said that people call this phenomenon – ECHO. It gives back everything one says. He further explained his son that this relationship applies to everything and in every aspects of life, that is why wise people say, "Life is a game of boomerang. Our thoughts, deeds and words return to us sooner or later, with astounding accuracy."

Many years ago. Two students of Stanford University in U.S.A were running short of fund and planned to make some money to pay their boarding and tuition fees by organizing a piano recital by great Ignacy Paderewski. Through his manager, the great pianist asked for $2000 as guarantee money. The duo agreed for the deal. However after the show was over, they could collect only $1600. The duo went straight to Paderewski and handed him $ 1600 along with a note of promise that they will earn and return the balance money at the earliest. Tearing off the note of promise, Paderewski said, "From $1600, you take out your expenses for organizing the show. From the balance you keep 10 per cent each for your efforts. Give me the rest."

After world war one, Paderewski, then premier of Poland was to arrange food for thousands of people suffering in his native land. He appealed for help to Herbert Hoover, the then in-charge of U.S. Food and Relief Bureau. Hoover immediately responded and tons and tons of foods were sent to Poland.

When Paderewski reached Hoover to thank him personally for the help, over shaking of hands Hoover said, "...... you don't remember it, you too helped me once when I was a student in the Stanford University and I was in trouble."

Life really gives back everything that is said or done. It is relevant to quote Dalai Lama in the above context. He said, "The law of actions and reactions is not exclusively for physics. It is also of human relations. If I act goodness, I will get goodness. If I act with evil, I will get evil....... The Universe is the echo of our actions and our thoughts."

5.9 Readiness is prerequisite to success

It is rightly said that failure to prepare is a preparation for failing. To achieve success in any specific discipline, preparation is a must.

Experts in any field make their tasks look easy because they persistently think and do a lot of hard work to master the fundamental of whatever they do.

All successful people believe in 'cause and effect', similar to the process of 'harvesting' where one reaps as he/she sows. So, they always prepare in advance. This enable them to avail opportunities when they surface. Abraham Lincoln became president of America from a humble background. His philosophy of life was, "If I had eight hours to chop down a tree, I would spend six hours sharpening my axe." In fact, he often would say, "I shall prepare. My chance will come someday."

Preparation is planning and practicing. Winston Churchill was a famous orator known around the world. But how many really knew about the 'behind the scene' preparation for those speeches? Hours after hours, he would continuously practice in front of a mirror, till he was satisfied with every line, intonation and gesticulation before he actually delivered the speech. His preparation was a hard work all the way.

Napoleon Bonaparte was very frank in confessing that if he appeared to be ever ready and equal to any occasion, it was because he had thought over matters long before he had undertaken them and had foreseen all eventualities. It is said that as a lieutenant, Napoleon often used to spend his leisure time in studying theories of artillery and related subjects, while his colleagues indulged in seeking pleasures. When asked if he believed in luck, he once said, "Yes, I do. I believe in bad luck. I believe I will always have it, and I plan accordingly."

People in general often fail to notice and appreciate the behind the scene preparation; that is why when one's preparedness meets with opportunity and culminate into success, they call him/her 'lucky'. Roger Bannister broke the four minutes barrier in 'mile race' not by luck. He made it happen through planned and structured hard work. Demosthenes became a famous orator not by chance. He had to prepare with lots of hard work and sacrifices.

The famous painter Holman Hunt was asked by an admirer how he could draw free hand circles as perfect as his. He replied, "All you need to do is, practice eight hours a day for forty years."

5.10 Self-pity is a progress breaker

Self pity can be defined as a state of mind in a perceived adverse situation where a person does not have the confidence or the ability to cope with it. It comes out of self-doubt and is the strongest evidence of a mind completely misdirected and is associated with the feelings that the person is a victim of events. It embraces pessimism.

Self-pity is a crippling emotional disease that severely distorts human perceptions of reality. It comes out of self-doubt and is a progress breaker. When a person fails to believe in himself, he fails to reach his potential.

Self-pity can be shunned through emotional maturity. Three basic factors influence emotional maturity are:

(a)   Ability to face reality.

(b)   Ability to relate with other.

(c)   Willingness to be honest with self.

The above can be developed through conscious efforts and experiences.

In 1962, a team of four enthusiastic British musicians failed in their audition test by Decca Recording Company. While rejecting them, one of the executives of the company said that their performance was unimpressive and the use of their main instrument - 'Guitar', was becoming obsolete. The group neither gave up singing nor did they stop using Guitar; eventually they established themselves as "Beetles" throughout the world of music.

Sidney Poiter, after his first audition, was told by his casting Director, "Why don't you stop wasting others time and go out and wash dishes or something?" He did not lose heart. Instead of brooding on self-pity and resigning to 'poor luck', he concentrated on his strength and ironed out his deficiencies and eventually established himself as a great Hollywood film actor.

Chapter Six

Decision Making Considerations

Thinking faculty plays important role in decision making. Upgraded knowledge, willingness to face problems outright, avoiding delays and fixing priorities are requisites for good decision making. To avoid erroneous result, decisions must never be taken in a disturbed state of mind.

Conviction makes one courageous and committed towards a task on hand and helps him/her in freezing decisions. These aspects are discussed separately in chapter seven.

6.1 Selection from many alternatives

Decision making basically is a process of selecting an option from various alternatives by reducing uncertainties and doubts to a great extent. It involves the following activities.

(a) Understanding clearly the subject matter and gathering relevant information from different sources. This warrants patiently listening to ideas and suggestions from others.

(b) Analyzing all the available inputs with due considerations.

(c) Working out different alternative decisions with identification of possible constraints in each of the options.

(d) Working out remedial contingency plans against each of the identified constraints.

(e) Selecting the best implementable decision after considering the consequence of each option. If deemed fit, one can combine the best features of different alternatives worked out and firm up the final decision.

(f) A decision means nothing till it is put into practice. So, after the best implementable alternative is selected, one needs to ensure that everyone affected by the decision is explained properly what is going to happen and why, and the channel of communication with all concerned is kept open so that he/she can get proper feedback for subsequent corrective actions if required.

It implies from above that patience with application of thinking faculty is the key to decision making.

Patience is a companion of wisdom and is known as the proper usage of experience and knowledge. Like human body is built through physical exercises, patience can also be developed through conscious thinking, hard work and persistence. With patience,

(a)   one gets relieved of stress,

(b)   exercises control on emotions with ease and poise even in difficult situations,

(c)   sees the big picture and,

(d)   makes proper assessment and deliberates before taking a decision.

The above reduce the chances of making a big mistake. Patience is a valuable human trait. Even though apparently it may appear to be passive, it is an active, purposeful and necessary form of self-discipline without which many of human decisions would be counter-productive. Benjamin Franklin succinctly said, "He that can have patience can have what he will."

With patience and application of thinking faculty, one

(a)   does not get easily perturbed or provoked.

(b)   can understand, analyze and assess things in the right perspective.

(c)   does not easily lose focus on the ultimate objective.

(d)   can use his/her intelligence to the maximum before taking a decision even under difficult circumstances.

One day, a man while returning home with his monthly wages was caught by an armed robber on a deserted street. The robber asked him to surrender whatever valuables he had. Thinking for a while, the man said, "Take everything I have but please do me a favour. Put a bullet through my hat so that when I go home I can show that and tell my wife that all my money had been snatched by a robber and she believes me." The robber obliged. The man then took out his coat and asked the robber, "Please do me another favour. Please shoot a number of holes through my coat so that I can tell her that I did put up a resistance and fought with the robber before surrendering." The robber obliged again. "And now..." continued the man. Interrupting, the robber said, "Sorry, no more holes. I'm out of bullet." "That's all I wanted to know!" shot back the man. The man then told the robber, "Return me back my money and some more for the hat and coat that you've ruined or I'll beat you black and blue!" The robber threw down the money and ran.

6.2 It is important to get started first

Instead of waiting and watching for the right time, to get started with a decision is very important in any venture. Nobody ever gets absolutely ready for any job or activity in life. Even before a 'presentation', irrespective of how many times one has written and memorized it, he/she always feels, "If only I had a little more time."

Madan Mohan Malaviya the eminent Indian scholar and patriot had a vision of establishing a Hindu University in Banaras. During the twenty-first Congress session held in Banaras, he convinced all the dignitaries present about the need of such a University and finally got his proposal approved. To start with, though he had no clue about the source of land and fund availability for the project, he never lost focus on his objective. For raising fund, he toured the whole of the country and collected donations from all cross sections of people. When approached, the Raja of Banaras gifted a plot of land for the entire project in the bank of holy river the Ganges. Later, the Maharaja of Darbhanga was so pleased with his work that he not only donated handsomely but also pledged to work for the noble cause for the rest of his life. On fourth February 1916, the foundation stone of the University was laid by the Viceroy and Governor General of India and the University was finally established.

The above demonstrates that when one gets started, even out of nothing and out of no way he/she makes a way to move towards his/her goal. It is relevant here to quote Ratan Tata, the ex chief of Tata Group. He said, "I don't believe in taking right decision....... I take decisions and then make them right........."

Everything in this world starts from a scratch. Even ace cricketer Sachin Tendulkar who has already scored more than 15,000 runs in test cricket by end of 2011, started his test career with zero runs against his name. It is relevant here to quote Zig Zagler. He said, "One does not have to be great to start, but one must start to become great."

To get started, sometimes one needs to break a deadlock in the mind between different options. Here decision on intuition comes into play. In intuitive decisions, no logic or reasoning is applied; it is based purely on years of experience and belief.

6.3 Hesitation in freezing a decision

Decision making is mandatory. Nothing moves without it. Inability to take decision often makes a person doubtful, anxious and anguished. These cause accumulation of problems, worries and aggression which eventually culminate even into physical ailments.

In section 6.1, it has been mentioned that one has to be patient and thoughtful in decision making. This however does not mean that one can take inordinate time to freeze decisions. Indecision always brings its own delays and days are lost lamenting over lost days. Along with delays, opportunities often get lost.

It is said that opportunity always comes in disguise and unless one is prepared to grab, it gets lost. Once lost, it never comes back again. Alexander the Great once visited the studio of a sculptor in

Athens. Seeing a statue with covered face and wings in the feet, he enquired, "What is its name?"

The sculptor replied, "Opportunity."

Alexander asked, "Why is its face covered?"

The sculptor said, "Because people rarely see opportunity when it passes before them."

Alexander asked, "But why do the feet have wings?"

The sculptor replied, "Because once it flies, it won't come back."

It is the vacillating mind which cause delays in decision making on various pretexts like, "Analyzing and reviewing all the considerations again and again", "Busy in other activities", "Observing and studying the environment for smooth implementation of action plans" etc. In the process, lots of valuable time gets lost. People who keep saying that they are busy, invariably do not find time. Those who say that they will do it tomorrow, almost certainly fail to do it the next day.

There is also a brand of people known as 'I told you so'. They can't zero in firmly on a decision. Seeing the result they either take credit and say, "I told you so" or discredit others and say, "I told you so." They seldom take responsibility, and in spite of the fact that they cause unnecessary delays in decision making, they always think and claim that they are right.

Hesitating tendency to freeze a decision is caused mainly because of one's thinking that in the event a decision goes wrong, he/she will be attached to the stigma of 'failure' or rejection. It is often seen that when one thinks too much but fails to take any action, fear makes its home within him/her. Since decisions are made based on past experience, knowledge, relevant gathered information, future anticipations and expectations, depending on the accuracy of all these inputs and precision of the analysis and subsequent overall considerations, a decision may sometime go wrong. This is very natural. In fact, it is inevitable during the growth of any individual. One does not have to feel hopeless or depressed under the above circumstances. Even Albert Einstein said, "If someone feels that he had never made a mistake, it means that he had never tried anything new in his life." A wrong decision never makes a person a failure for the entire life.

6.4 A mistake does not ruin entire life

Those who have the crippling desire to be appreciated by everyone for every decision he/she takes, must keep it in mind that all decisions cannot be correct all the time.

During a deliberation on decision making, a speaker holding a thousand rupees note asked the delegates, "Who would like to get this note?" Hands started getting raised. He then crumpled the note and asked, "Who still wants it?" Hands again started getting raised. He then dropped the note on the ground and started to grind it into the floor with his shoes. Finally, picking up the note from the floor, he again asked, "Who still wants it?" Hands still went up because the note did not lose its value.

Then turning towards the delegates, the speaker said, "Like the note has not lost its value, your value also will not be lost if you make a wrong decision. Remember, even Henry Ford forgot to put a reverse gear in his first car."

The speaker further went on to say, "A president of a bank was once asked by a journalist, 'Sir, what is the secret of your success?' The President replied, 'Two Words.' The journalist shot back, 'Sir what are those two words?' The president replied, 'Good decisions.' The journalist then asked, 'Sir, how do you make good decisions?' The president replied, 'One word'. The journalist then asked, 'Sir, what is that single word?' The president replied, 'Experience.' The journalist then asked, 'Sir, how do you get experience?' The president replied, 'Two words.' The journalist finally asked, 'Sir, what are those two words?' The president replied, 'Bad decisions.'" So, even if a decision goes wrong, one can learn from it.

Mistakes, when they happen are very painful. But when one accepts it and learns from it, he/she becomes wiser with enhance confidence.

6.5   Different aids to decision making

Broadly speaking, the following aid in decision making:

(a)   Inspiration drawn from the features of Lord Ganesh.

(b)   Updated knowledge/information base.

(c)   Control on ego and anger.

The features of Lord Ganesh send inspiring messages. It tells every individual to listen and concentrate more, talk less, think inquisitively and be cool with focus fixed on the goal.

Lord Ganesh

(a)   His big head tells people to think big and think profitably.

(b)   His narrow eyes tell people to concentrate deeply and focus on 'goal'.

(c)   His long nose tells people to poke around inquisitively to learn more.

(d)   His small mouth tells people to talk less.

(e)   His big ears tell people to listen patiently to new ideas and suggestions.

Knowledge and information are very vital inputs in decision making. They need to be continuously updated. One therefore needs to learn to live with mental door unlocked to welcome fresh ideas/suggestions.

Discussion is a very common media through which one can learn new things and expand his/her knowledge/information base which is so vital in decision making. If two persons have a rupee coin each and they exchange their coins, they will continue to have one coin each. But, if they have one idea each and they exchange them through discussions, they will have two ideas each.

Uncontrolled ego and anger have adverse effect in decision making. When influenced by ego, discussions often stretch into the zone of argument where winning becomes more important than drawing conclusion on the subject on which discussion start initially. Inflated ego causes anger.

There is a basic difference between discussion and argument. During argument,

(a)   ego takes centre stage,

(b)   lot of heat is generated associated with display of frayed temper and high pitch vocal cord and,

(c)   establishing superiority by winning at any cost and exploring the ignorance of other becomes the priority.

During discussion,

(a)   with exchange of knowledge and backing of sound logic, important issues come to the surface. This makes decision making easier.

(b)   participants being open minded, the mutual emphasis is on settling what is right rather than establishing who is right.

Issues of importance bypassed or ignored out of ego/anger often prove to be costly in the long run. Facts after all continue to exist even if they are bypassed or ignored.

6.6   Decision making in unstable mind

Once while walking along with few of his followers, Lord Buddha stopped in front of a lake. Being thirsty, he asked one of his disciples to bring him a glass of water. As he was going to bring water, he saw a bullock cart crossing the lake and some people were seen washing their clothes. The water looked very muddy and turbid. So, the disciple came back empty handed and told Buddha that the water was not fit for drinking.

After sometime, Buddha again asked the same disciple to bring him water for drinking. As he went, the disciple was surprised to see clear water with all mud settled underneath. Considering it to be fit for drinking, he immediately collected some water in a pot and brought the same for his Lord.

Seeing the water, Buddha looked up at the disciple and said, "See what you did to make the water clean. You let it be, and the mud settled down on its own and then you got clear water." Lord Buddha further said, "Your mind is also like that! When it is disturbed, just let it be. Give it a little time. It will settle down on its own. You don't have to put in any effort to calm it down. It will happen automatically."

The above sends the message that in a disturbed state of mind, human thinking faculty is also likely to be in a state of imbalance. Any decision taken in that state of mind can lead to erroneous result.

6.7   Kept pending, problems get bigger

Swami Vivekananda was once walking along a footpath in Benaras. All on a sudden, he turned back and noticed that few monkeys were following him. He got scared and started moving faster. Seeing the monkeys still following him at faster pace, he started running. Watching his plight, an old passerby caught him by his hand and asked him to turn back, face and chase the monkeys. Swamiji did that and the monkeys fled away.

The above is the reality of life. By running away from problems, one does not get respite; the problems keep running after him/ her. Kept alive, problems always have tendency to raise their head again and again with multiplied adverse effects. The wisest decision is to face them outright and neutralize/resolve them in the early stage of identification. It is rightly said, "The biggest problem in the world could have been solved when it was small."

Azim Premji, the chairman of WIPRO, in one of his deliberations to the students of IIT, Delhi, on 12th August 2006 said, "When you face a great challenge,

(a) you can run away from it,

(b) push it on to someone else or,

(c) just plain roll-up your sleeves and face it head on."

He further said, "I have always chosen to take charge. In the long run, I found it the easiest option of all..............The first thought that came to my mind when I stepped into Wipro factory at Amalner over four decades ago was, 'Take charge'. I was 21 and had spent the last few years in Stanford University at California, U.S.A. Many people advised me to take up a nice, cushy job rather than face the challenges of running a hydrogenated oil business. Looking back, I am glad I decided to take charge instead..............
It is a small voice that tells you where to go when you feel lost. If you believe in that voice, you believe in yourself. You can either amplify the voice to make it the purpose of your life or you can discount it and turn it off. I believe that at the end of the day, our destiny is too precious to leave the choice to someone else..........
..............."

No problem can withstand the assault of sustained thinking and actions. The thinking and the follow up actions however has to be initiated with an open mind. Albert Einstein very candidly said, "No solution can be obtained to a problem if one continues to be in the same level of thinking when it was created."

To face and counter any problem, one has to be –

(a) big enough to admit his/her mistake when the problem is created.

(b) smart enough to learn from it and,

(c) strong enough to implement corrective measures in time.

6.8 Dogmatism effect decision making

Buzzards have the ability to fly. But because of their habits, they need space to run before flying. When put in six feet by eight pens with open top, because of not finding space to run, they don't even attempt to fly and remain prisoners for life in those enclosures.

The 'bats' fly around at night. However, because of their habit, they cannot take off from a level place. If they are placed on the floor of a flat ground, all they can do is shuffle about painfully and helplessly till they reach some slight elevation from which they can throw themselves into the air. Then, at once, they take off like a flash.

A bumblebee, when dropped into an open tumbler, will be there till it dies, unless it is taken out. It does not see the means of escape at the top, but persists in trying to find some way out through the sides near the bottom. If it ultimately does not find one, it completely destroys itself.

The above phenomenon of stubbornly holding on to a belief (dogmatism) is prevailing in human behaviour too. Dogmatism is characterized by rigidity, defensiveness and biasness. Instead of looking for a better alternative, many remain dogmatic with old ideas and experiences in trying circumstances and get devastated. In some cases they even get destroyed.

Alexander Graham Bell said, "When one door closes, another door opens; but we so often look so long and so regretfully upon the closed door, that we do not see the one which is open for us." Depending on situations, one needs to come out of 'dogma' and be flexible during 'consideration' before a decision is made. It should always be kept in mind that if the same things are done the same way the same result will follow irrespective of how many times one does it.

6.9 Responses are wiser than reactions

In demanding situations, one's emotion generally gets triggered and takes centre stage and inhibits his/her ability to pause and cool down. Pausing and cooling down before a decision is taken has the potential to take one beyond 'reacting' into the more subtle and creative realm of responding; it makes one feel the feet on the ground, air on the skin and listen to the response from within.

While responding, one evaluates with a calm mind and does whatever is most appropriate and thus controls emotions and actions. While reacting, one is likely to act on impulse and bring in more of complications. Reactions are always instinctive, whereas responses are backed by thoughtful consideration.

There was a farmer in a village. He had the misfortune of owing a large amount of money to a money lender. He could not pay back the money lender in time. In return, the money lender proposed to marry his daughter. The proposal was not acceptable to the farmer. The money lender then suggested and convinced the villager that a committee headed by a Chief decide the matter and put forward his following proposals.

He said that he would put a black pebble and a white pebble into an empty money bag and the girl will have to pick up one.

(a) If she picked the black pebble, she would become his wife and her father's debt would be forgiven.

(b)   If she picked the white pebble, she did not have to marry him and her father's debt would still be forgiven.

(c)   But if she refused to pick a pebble, her father would be put to jail.

On the day of the judgment, all the villagers along with the money lender were standing on a pebble strewn path in the farmer's field. As they talked, the money lender bent over and picked up two black pebbles. He then asked the girl to pick a pebble from the bag.

In spite of watching everything the money lender did, the girl did not react immediately. She responded after some time with her strategy made. She put her hand into the money bag and drew out a pebble. Without looking at it, she consciously fumbled and let it fall onto the pebble strewn path where it immediately became lost among all other pebbles. Pretending to chide herself, the girl immediately told the money lender, "Never mind, if you look into the bag for the one that is left, you will be able to tell the colour of the pebble which dropped from my hand." Since the one left in the bag was black, the money lender was forced to accept that she had picked up the white one. He did not dare to admit his dishonesty in front of the village gathering and kept silent.

The girl changed what seemed to be an impossible situation into an extremely advantageous one through her response after keen observation and thoughtful considerations on the spot.

6.10 Importance of priority fixation

It has been mentioned earlier that proper utilization of time is very important in decision making. Time once lost cannot be retrieved and with it, opportunity also gets lost.

Time is like flow of streams of water in a river. The stream of water that passes once never passes again. One therefore has to be disciplined to do things in an orderly sequence instead of acting impulsively as per his/her moods and fancies. This calls for fixation of priorities.

What prioritization is, has been very clearly demonstrated by a professor while delivering a lecture to his students as mentioned underneath. Before delivering the lecture, the professor put the following items in a table.

(a) A transparent jar and few golf balls.

(b) Few bags of sand, pebbles and two cups of coffee.

He first took the jar and filled it up with golf balls and asked all the students after shaking the jar, "Can some more golf balls be filled in?" The students replied, "No, the jar is full." He then picked up the bags of pebbles and poured them into the jar to fill up the interstices between the golf balls. He kept on shaking the jar while pouring the pebbles till the students said no more pebbles could be put in. He then picked up the bags of sand and started filling the jar so that the interstices between the pebbles could be filled in. While pouring in sand, he was constantly shaking the jar till the students were convinced and said that nothing more could go inside the jar. He then picked up two cups of coffee and started pouring them inside the jar. When the coffee was sipped in by the sand, he asked the students, "Is the jar still full?" The students burst into laughter. As the laughter subsided, the professor said, "This jar represents your life. The golf balls are the important things, the pebbles are the other things that matter and sand is everything else – the small stuff."

With a pause, he further said, "If you first put the sand in the jar, there will be no room left for the pebbles and golf ball. The same goes for your life too – you have to set your priorities. If you spend all time and energy on the small 'stuff' and the 'other things', you will never have time for the things that are of more importance."

Cups of coffee in the above represents that no matter how full one's life may seem, there is always room for a cup of coffee with a friend.

Chapter Seven

Commitment Drives

Commitment is a pledge to do/achieve something irrespective of circumstances. It warrants lots of sacrifices. Commitment leads to perseverance, optimism, resoluteness and assertiveness. It drives people towards becoming 'winners'.

7.1 Commitment simply is a pledge

In the game of football, to 'score', each team has identified goal posts at fixed positions. During the course of a match, each team is focused towards opponent's goal posts for 'scoring' by employing various strategies. For ease of scoring or stopping the opponent from scoring, at no stage of the game the teams can change the positions of the goal posts at the opponent's end or self-end respectively. In human life too, when a goal is set, one has to remain focused towards; it cannot be changed. The strategy to approach the goal however can be altered depending on circumstances. Remaining focused and involved under all circumstances towards a goal till the end is called commitment. Commitment basically is a force that binds an individual, a team or an organization to a course of action of relevance to one or more targets.

Commitment is a conscious decision (a pledge or an understanding without any written documentation) to stick to 'something' in spite of having other options.

Keroly Takacs (refer section 3.4) was a right handed pistol shooter of Hungary. While representing his country in 1939, an army grenade exploded in his right hand. Such was his exemplary commitment that after that incident, he started practicing shooting left handed and nine years later he won his first gold medal in rapid fire pistol at the London Olympics and won another gold medal at the next Olympic held at Helsinki in 1952 (all with left hand shooting).

Life tests everyone for his/her level of commitments. The greatest rewards are reserved for those who demonstrate 'a never ending commitment' till they achieve their goal.

7.2 Interest/promise/commitment

Commitment is not to be confused with 'interest' or 'promise'. An interested person does something only when circumstances permit, but a committed person always goes after the end result of a task on hand without accepting any excuses on the way.

Peter Drucker says, "Unless commitment is made, there are only promises and hopes; and no plans." A promise basically is a statement of intent and commitment transforms the promise into reality (irrespective of circumstances).

Committed individuals value moral correctness more than the personal benefits. This is reflected in their behaviour and actions. It is rightly said that commitment produces character with integrity and empathy that –

(a)   gets one out from the bed,

(b)   moves him/her into actions and,

(c)   disciplines him/her to follow through till his/her goal is achieved.

7.3 Conviction makes people committed

Conviction is a firmly held belief or opinion. Unlike preference which gives way under pressure, conviction push people to become stronger in mind and not wilt under any pressure. It makes people committed towards a task. Famous boxer Muhammad Ali often said, "It is the repetition of affirmations that leads to belief. And once that belief becomes a deep conviction, things begin to happen."

Since inception, Indian Iron and Steel Company, Burnpur, had been making steels with the old 'DUPLEX' technology (combination of acid Bessemer converter and basic open hearth furnace). Considering it to be uneconomic, the operation of acid Bessemer converters were discontinued since 1988. Between 1988 and 1999, to make steel, the shop utilized the six open hearth furnaces with introduction of top lancing facilities. This change in process was associated with drop in shop productivity and high incidences of furnace wall and bottom breakouts for which the operating personnel of steel melting shop were always held responsible.

In early 1999, the newly appointed Managing Director of IISCO, Burnpur looked at the persisting problems from different angles. He had thread bare discussions about various aspects of the shop operations with the steel melting shop collectives. Following that he consulted the steel experts from other units of Steel Authority of India Limited and had detailed discussions with the senior executives of the plant. He was convinced that the open hearth furnaces initially designed for duplex systems were not technically fit to be operated with high metallurgical and thermal load associated with the scrap and hot metal charge with top lancing. Out of conviction he immediately took the following daring decisions.

(a) Open hearth furnaces would be replaced by twin hearth furnace technology. Two open hearth furnaces would immediately be scrapped and dismantled and the first twin hearth furnace would be erected in that area.

(b) The project division of IISCO will work with engineers from Bhillai Steel plant (an unit of SAIL) to indigenously design a 2 x 110 tons twin hearth furnace which could utilize the flue systems of the dismantled pair of open hearth furnaces and the available facilities in casting bay like cranes, ladles and teeming systems.

(c)   The new furnace would be brought into operation by the year end with maximum use of in-house facilities.

Since the company's financial health was not sound at that point in time, after conveying his decisions, he convinced the officer's association and employee's unions that in case of exigency during construction period, he would realize money from the employee's salary and reimburse the same after completion of furnace construction activities.

Immediately a pair of open hearth furnaces was dismantled. The engineers of IISCO and Bhillai steel plant completed on war footing the design parameters of the furnace which would fit into the existing facilities of the shop like furnace flue systems, logistics of materials, teeming arrangements etc. Fabrications of structural members were completed mostly through in house work. Furnace erection was completed as scheduled and first heat was tapped on the 26th day of December 1999.

The venture was not only successful from quick 'concept to commissioning point of view', the performance of the twin hearth furnace justified the conviction and commitment of a man who stood against all odds and completed his ambitious plan that saved the company from immediate collapsing during that period.

7.4   Conviction/commitment/courage

Conviction leads to commitment and makes one courageous to face any eventualities in his/her effort to do something good. Courage can be explained as:

(a)   standing up for what one believes in without worrying about the opinion of others even if it is a new step or a path that nobody had taken or thought of in the past,

(b)   having full confidence, owning responsibility and remaining unmoved in the face of disappointment with the belief that things will ultimately get better even if they get worse to start with,

(c) setting a goal, sticking to it even in the face of impediment, and stopping at nothing till the objectives are achieved.

In the above case of reference (section7.3) courage arising out of conviction and commitment of the Managing Director of reference was instrumental in the fast and successful completion of the project against heavy odds.

The project did not have a smooth sailing at all. Immediately, after the first pair of open hearth furnaces was dismantled, order was placed for procurement of structural materials for fabrication jobs (on the basis of ongoing design parameters). The shops were gearing up to take up in phases the fabrication activities of the structural members whose drawings were complete. At this stage, the Managing Director was intimated by the SAIL board that the 'go ahead' signal for the entire project would be granted only after the total design parameters of the proposed twin hearth furnace were completed and approved by a 'competent design bureau'.

In spite of above and also being aware that for easy reference there was no 2 x 110 tons twin hearth furnace which ever operated or even existed anywhere in the world till then, the Managing Director had the courage to stand by his engineers and encourage them to complete the design parameters on war footing. A competent design bureau eventually approved the engineering details without any correction or additions.

Before getting the official 'go ahead' signal from SAIL board, the Managing Director had to withstand lots of criticisms for dismantling two running open hearth furnaces as this reduced the availability of operating furnaces in the shop at that point in time. He however had been unruffled by the circumstances. When the SAIL board finally accorded official approval, various job activities were in different stages of advancement. This was the main reason which enabled the plant to complete the 'construction' and 'erection' within a short period of time. All his actions finally resulted in saving of enormous amount of time for the entire project.

The above reminds author Robert Greene. He said, "Always be audacious. Audacity will often get you into trouble, but even more audacity will get you out."

To make a better tomorrow, committed people with conviction take courageous decisions against odds even if it involves elements of risks and criticisms to start with. And they often succeed.

7.5   Commitment warrants sacrifices

Commitment warrants sacrifices and willingness to accept hardships. Sacrificing some of the things one loves in order to focus on what can have the biggest impact on him/her in the long run is not an easy task.

The famous Swedish tennis player Bjorn Borg had stated that during his active playing days, he dedicated all his 'energy and time' to continually hone and sharpen his skills. He was so committed, involved and engrossed with his practice schedules that he often said no to his friends, family and others for any form of entertainment. Nothing came on platters to Bjorn Borg.

It has been mentioned earlier (refer section 3.5) that during the Brooklyn bridge building project, when Washington Roebling was struck by a disaster, he lost his ability to walk and talk. Though he was physically unable to communicate anything even through sign language, his memory and mind was as sharp as before.

Subsequently, his wife established a code of communication between them, and persuaded her husband to start his dream project of bridge construction again. For thirteen long years she remained totally committed to her husband's dream project as the only link of communication between the field engineers and her husband. She toiled untiringly and totally sacrificed her personal life, till the construction and erection of the bridge was completed.

Brooklyn Bridge today stands tall not only as an example of motivation and indomitable spirit of Roebling father and son, but also as a tribute to exemplary commitment, hard work and sacrifice of Washington Roebling's wife.

7.6   Commitment and perseverance

When hard work does not lead towards achievement of a desired objective, it gives enough of indications that the 'process of approach' needs to be reviewed for necessary modifications on the principle of 6Ps (Proper & Prior Planning Prevents Poor Performance). Committed people always take cue from such indications and make preparations by implementing corrective strategies during their subsequent effort.

In the year 2000, circumstances in the steel melting shop of Indian Iron and Steel Company, Burnpur warranted that the repair schedule of the only twin hearth furnace be drastically reduced. Accordingly, the shop collectives planned to bring down the duration of the next 'short roof repair' of the furnace to fifteen shifts as opposed to the prevailing norm of twenty-four shifts. Industrial engineers were asked to prepare a fifteen shift repair schedule allocating time slices to different activities as percentage of the total repair time based on previous trends. The repair however could be completed in twenty-two shifts.

The commitment of the 'collectives' however persuaded them to continue reviewing and exploring possibilities of squeezing the timing of various activities with introduction of new ideas and strategies during their subsequent 'repair' efforts. Their perseverance finally paid them dividend. On their fifth attempt, they not only made it happen but also established the norms and sequencing of activities to be performed to complete the repair within fifteen shifts on regular basis.

7.7 Commitment/optimism/resoluteness

Commitment makes people optimistic and resolute. Optimism can be defined as the tendency to expect the best outcome or dwell on the most helpful aspects of any given situation and resoluteness is the firm intention to achieve the desired end.

In 2006, the collieries of IISCO Steel plant, Steel Authority of India limited were going through a very lean period. The two operating coking coal mines, Chasnala and Jitpur were producing an average of four rakes (each rake carrying around 3500 metric tons of coal) of washed coal per month, while the steel plant required 8/9 rakes per month. The additional coal required by the plant had to be cash purchased from external sources. The team at that point in time practically reconciled to the fact that nothing better could be achieved under the prevailing circumstances.

Towards the end of the year, there was a change in the management at the top. The new chief was a committed personality with full of optimism and resoluteness. He was a firm believer of the philosophy of Norman Vincent Peale who always said, "If you expect the best, you will be the best..... Learn to expect, not to doubt. In so doing, you bring everything into realm of possibility" and all along tried to impress this spirit on his team members. On quick observation and review, he identified that –

(a)   coals were available in the mines,

(b)   the washery unit at Chasnala was underutilized, and

(c)   available heavy earth moving machineries were underutilized because of shortage of machine operators.

Immediately, he expressed his desire to raise the production level to ten rakes and above. He urged the employees of all cross sections to come up with ideas so that this level of production could be achieved in the short as well as in the long term. He promised the team full support and assured them that if any of their decisions misfired, he himself would shoulder the responsibility. People initially took his words very lightly. However driven by his commitment, the employees quickly realized that he meant business and joined hands with him to make things happen.

When suggestions started pouring in, he engaged a 'core group' to analyze every proposal for necessary scrutiny before putting up for approval of the competent authority. He even persuaded the officer's association and employees unions to get involved in the thinking as well as implementation process. Within three months, myths were broken and long standing problematic issues started getting resolved. The following proposals were approved by the competent authority and the Identified action plans were implemented on war footing.

(a)   Shifting of unauthorized occupants of huts from West Quarry, Chasnalla to a decoaled area with suitable compensation to the inhabitants.

(For a long time, around four hundred thirty odd unauthorized families were occupying different parts of west quarry forcing total suspension of open cast mining on the ground of human safety. With batch-wise shifting of these occupants, open cast mining to reclaim million tons of unrecovered coal could start immediately).

(b)   Tying up with another coal company, M/S Bharat Coking Coal Limited to use part of their raw coal through the 'washery' at Chasnala.

(Apart from increasing the throughput of coal in the washery, it enabled the company to save on immediate cash outflow along with a profit margin during conversion of raw coal to washed coal).

(c) Rationalization and reorganization of existing work force to create a 'pool' of heavy earth moving machine operators. They were subsequently trained.

(This enabled utilization of the idle mining equipments with immediate enhancement of production from the open cast mines).

After six months, the team raised their output to eight rakes per month and subsequently raised it further to ten rakes and above on consistent basis. With his outlook and philosophy, the new coal chief really made a big difference in the performance of the colliery unit.

The above reminds Dr. Walter Staples. He said, "Keep clearly in mind the desired outcome you want. Your mind will then ensure that you act and perform in such a way that you will bring this picture into reality."

7.8 Commitment/enthusiasm/assertiveness

Commitment keeps one's enthusiasm alive and makes him/her assertive. Enthusiasm is an activity or a subject that one is interested in or excited about and is considered to be the mother of all 'efforts'. It:

(a) is a switch which controls the power (one's capability),

(b) keeps one's interest intact instead of quitting in the face of problems,

(c) gives one courage to take risks needed for success,

(d) fuels motivation to make things happen,

(e) helps one to combat fear and worry,

(f)   is the hidden spring of endless energy,

(g)   is a force that can carry one from mediocrity to excellence,

(h)   can even rejuvenate the old.

The last four alphabets of the word 'enthusiasm' – 'iasm' stand for 'I AM SERIOUSLY MOTIVATED'.

Assertiveness can be defined as taking responsibility of any situation instead of looking towards other people or circumstances to shape the situation. With assertiveness, one listens to the call from his/her heart and actively takes charge and thereby controls his/her destiny.

It is his enthusiasm and assertiveness arising of commitment which fired John Logie Baird to organize and stick to his project of television invention in spite of facing every conceivable handicap. Before John Logie Baird, many renowned scientists had tried and failed in transmitting pictures by electric signals. He had a poor health and his financial position was equally bad. When he ran out of money, he had to sacrifice food and often was threatened of eviction by his land lord. To carry out his experimentation, he

(a)   procured a motor from a junk shop,

(b)   used a primitive projection lamp in an empty biscuit tin fitted with lenses purchased from an ordinary shop,

(c)   collected parts of discarded military wireless systems and other necessary materials for the project.

The entire technical jumble was held together by glue, string, sealing wax and electric wires. Nothing however could make any dent on his commitment. He eventually was successful and invented television in December 1941.

7.9 Commitment explores as well as creates

Commitment generates belief and drives people not only to explore but also to create solutions in 'crises'. Partial relining of blast furnace was carried out for the first time in India in no 3 blast furnace in ISP, SAIL, Burnpur in 2003. Two important steps involved in this project were –

(a) evacuation of 'nut coke' from the blast furnace to the cast house floor, and back loading them manually into skip boxes and,

(b) removing and dumping these skip boxes to a predetermined site by overhead crane.

During execution, it was noticed that even though shifting of the loaded skip boxes with nut coke by overhead crane to a predetermined place was very fast, manual loading of the skip boxes were taking exorbitant time (even after deployment of more manpower than initially planned). This caused jamming of cast house floor which adversely affected other repair activities because of space constraint. In spite of extensive brain storming, no solution to this problem could emerge immediately and the entire repair schedules looked threatened to get dislocated.

Next morning, after prolonged discussions, the team made a departure from conventional thinking and decided to lift a tyre mounted loader in the cast house to augment loading rate of skip boxes. Many laughed at the idea and others cautioned the team members against possible damage to the 'loader' while 'lifting'. The determined team however stuck to their decision and lifted the loader in the cast house floor in the forenoon.

As anticipated by the blast furnace collectives, 'loader' solved their problem on hand and enabled them to complete the entire repair schedules in time. The committed team, when faced with the unforeseen problem, analyzed the situation with a positive frame of mind and was courageous to take and implement an unconventional decision which had never been even thought of in the past. They eventually were able to create the circumstances they wanted.

George Bernard Shaw was spot on in his realization that the people who get on in this world are those who get up and look for the circumstances they wanted. If they cannot find them, they make them.

7.10 Commitment to excellence has no limit

It is said that if one is content with the best he/she has achieved, he/she will never be able to extract the best he/she is capable of. While being interviewed by a British press after completing 14,000 runs in test cricket, Sachin Tendulkar said, "I am really focusing now on how I can get to the next level as a batsman. How I can get even more competitive? How I can get even more consistent? How can I get better?" Commitment to excellence has no limit.

In the popular Zee Bangla T.V. Show, Dadagiri Part one, Saurav Ganguly, the former captain of Indian cricket team, was asked by the young participants as well as their parents to share some of his experiences in life. During one of the episodes he said that even though he was good in cricket, football and studies, towards the later part of his school days he decided to concentrate only on cricket to make it his career. Subsequently, even though he was totally committed to continually hone his cricketing skills, he never imagined that he would represent India in 100 test matches which he eventually did. This is a testimony to Saurav Ganguly's belief that doing the best at this moment can put him in the best of place for the next moment.

Committed people on reaching a milestone set their next goal above their last achievement. In this way, they raise the level of their aspirations and achieve the same. They have unquenchable thirst for excellence with no bar on limit.

Chapter Eight

'Belief' Is Positiive Push

Thought accepted as truth is belief. It makes one feel that whatever he/she hopes for will actually happen. It spurs one to overcome adversity and makes him/her feel that even infirmity can be a blessing in disguise. Unlike reasoning, belief has no limits. It often pushes people beyond boundaries and enables him/her to do/achieve wonders.

8.1 Thought accepted as truth is 'belief'

Belief is a state of being where one is certain that his/her anticipation is going to be correct or that his/her selected course of action is the best and the most effective. It is basically a 'trust' on something not necessarily based on proof. Belief is a thought which makes one feel that whatever he/she hopes for will actually happen.

Sri Sri Ravi Shankar says, "Faith is a wealth. It gives strength and stability..........If you lack faith you have to pray for faith. Yet to pray, you need faith........There are three types of faith.

(a) Faith in yourself: Without faith in yourself, you think, 'I cannot do this'/'This is not for me'/'I shall never feel freedom in my life'.

(b) Faith in the world: You must have faith in the world or you cannot move an inch.

(c) Faith in divine: Have faith in divine and you will evolve."

Sri Sri Ravi Shankar further says, "All these faiths are connected. You must have all three for each to be strong. If you start doubting one, you are starting doubting everything."

Swami Vivekananda said, "The history of the world is the history of a few men who had faith in themselves. As soon as a man loses faith in himself, death comes. Believe first in yourself and then in God." Without 'belief', one cannot focus on the course to victory in any journey.

Belief is very powerful and is a pillar that supports all acts of creations and often makes one free of worries and anxieties. It is rightly said, "The beginning of anxiety is the end of faith, and the true faith is the end of anxiety."

8.2 Belief supplies power of resilience

Norman Vincent Peale said, "Anybody can keep going when the going is good but some extra ingredient is needed to enable you to keep fighting when it seems that everything is against you. Faith supplies the staying power. It contains dynamic to keep one going when the going is hard."

It is the belief and acceptance of the fact that good and bad days are part of life which helps one to regain composure to move forward with confidence even in adverse situations.

Arthur Ashe, the legendary Wimbledon tennis champion, was dying of AIDS which he got due to infected blood he received during his heart surgery earlier. From world over he received letters of concern and sympathy from his fans and well wishers. One of his fans wrote, "Why God had to select such a bad disease for you?"

Arthur Ashe replied, "The world over, fifty million children start playing tennis, but only five million learn to play. Five lacks learn professional tennis, out of which only fifty thousand join the 'circuit'. Five thousand reach to grand slam level, but only fifty reach the Wimbledon. Four reach the semi-final, and two reach the final. After winning the Wimbledon Championship, holding the trophy I never asked God - Why me?" He further said, " If I were to say, 'God why me?' about the bad things, then I should have said, 'God why me?' about the good things that happened in my life......I had good days and bad days. My ratio of good days to bad days is about six to one. I don't think anybody of my age would be able to go through with no bad days."

Birds build their nests over a period of time by collecting materials from distant places. However, their nests at different stage of building often get destroyed by a storm or by an act of human or by animals. Sometimes, this happens after nests are made or even when eggs are hatched. They however never stop at that. They continue to be positive and keep singing and building again because of their belief - "That's the way we have to live."

Belief does not make things easy but certainly helps one to become realistic.

8.3   Belief amplifies good things in life

Belief amplifies good things in life and spurs people to be always positive irrespective of circumstances. Jessica Cox is the middle of three siblings of an American father and a Filipino mother in Tuscan, Arizona. She was born with no hands and the Doctors could not explain this rare congenital condition. Sonogram and other prenatal tests did not reveal any defect. However, with her belief and indomitable spirit she overrides what she lacks physically. She is proficient in dancing, graduated in psychology and is a double black belt in Tai-know-Do. By using her feet, she can write, swim, brush her hair, talk on the phone, drive a car, operate a computer and fly an aircraft.

Jessica Cox declares with confidence, "I highly encourage people with disabilities to consider flying...........it helps reverse the stereo type belief that people with disabilities are powerless into the belief that they are powerful and capable of setting high goals and achieve them."

Doug Landis of U.S.A was born a normal child. Unfortunately, while still in school, he met with an accident during a wrestling bout. His body was paralyzed from neck below. Seeing him sitting in front of T.V and idling time, his brother coaxed him to do something by putting a pencil in his mouth. Through practice,

practice and practice, he responded in affirmative and developed his own method of drawing which is appreciated worldwide and is known as 'Mouth Art'. He does his art by holding the pencil by his teeth and using his mouth as an artist's hand. He uses his neck to move the pencil. He is famous for sketching of animals with fading out style. They represent animal habitats which are getting destroyed and concurrently becoming extinct. Depending on the size, he takes around 40 hours to 200 hours to draw an image he plans.

Doug Landis believes and says, ".....every one of us has hidden talent within ourselves." These talents need to be explored and utilized.

The above reminds Helen Keller. She said, "Face your deficiencies and acknowledge them; but do not let them master you. Let them teach you patience.........When we do the best we can, we never know what miracle is wrought in our life........"

8.4 Belief with courage breaks boundaries

Helen Keller was born a normal child. At the age of nineteen months, she contacted a disease described by doctors as "acute congestion of stomach and the brain." Though the illness did not last for a long time, it left her deaf and blind even before she learned to speak.

At her age of seven, Anne Sullivan, a twenty years old graduate of Perkins School for the blind became her private tutor through the sympathetic interest of Alexander Graham Bell who was then working with deaf children.

Sullivan initially tried to teach her to connect objects with letters by spelling d-o-l-l in one hand while Helen was asked to hold a doll in the other hand. Even though she was willing to learn, Helen did not know that she was spelling a word or even that words existed. One fine day, Sullivan put one of Helen's hands under the flow of a stream of tap water and started spelling w - a - t - e - r first slowly and then rapidly into her other hand. Suddenly, she realized that water meant a cool substance flowing over her hand. Immediately she touched earth and demanded its letter name. By end of the night that day, she learned thirty words. She quickly learned all the alphabets, both manual and in raised print for blind readers, and gained facility in writing and reading.

At the age of ten, she came to know that a little deaf, dumb and blind girl in Norway acquired ability to speak. She immediately expressed her desire to learn to speak. Miss Sarah Fuller was appointed her first teacher for speech. Being a determined learner and using her persistence, she eventually became the first deaf, dumb and blind to graduate from a college and later established herself as a world famous speaker and author. She travelled worldwide, campaigned for civil rights, world peace, human dignity and women rights and authored many books and essays. She received numerous national as well as international awards for her work for the services of mankind.

Hellen Keller never regretted her deficiencies. She always believed and said,

(a) "Doubts and mistrust are the mere panic of timid imagination."

(b) "Self-pity is our worst enemy and if we yield to it, we can never do anything good in this world."

After her death, in his eulogy, Senator Lister Hill of Alabama expressed the feelings of the whole world when he said of Helen Keller, "She will live on, one of the immortal names, not born to die. Her spirit will endure as long as man can read and stories can be told of the woman who showed the world that there are no boundaries to courage and faith."

8.5   Belief turns even infirmity into blessings

It has been mentioned earlier how Thomas Alva Edison became short of hearing after being slapped by a train guard.

In subsequent years, he referred to this infirmity as a blessing in disguise as it shut him out from the noise of the world and enabled him to concentrate on his work. He did not even know what gossips were and gave the following simple message to the youth, "Genius is 99% hard work and 1% intelligence."

There was a young boy who lost an arm in a car accident. He started taking training from a Japanese master in Judo. During the initial three months, the master taught him only one move. Being curious the boy one day asked his master, Should not I be learning more moves?' "No, the one you have learned is the only move you need to know. Master it", said the coach. Being obedient and trusting the coach, the boy continued to train harder.

After few months, the boy took part in his first competitive tournament. Surprising everybody, the boy easily won his first two matches. In the third match, he had a very tough and strong opponent who was very impatient and was trying to put the boy down quickly. The boy however took advantage of his impatience and deftly used his one move to win the match and reach the final. In the final, the boy appeared to be a mismatch to his opponent who was stronger, bigger and more experienced. During the bout, being concerned that the boy might get hurt, the referee called a time out. In fact, he was about to stop the match when the coach intervened and said, "Let him continue."

After the match resumed, the boy's opponent made a critical mistake: he dropped his guard. Instantly, the boy used the only move he knew and pinned him. The boy became the champion.

On their way home, the boy and his coach reviewed every move in each and every match. The boy summoned up courage and asked his coach, "Sir, how could I win the entire tournament with only one move?" The coach replied, "Your win can be attributed to two things,

(a)   you have almost mastered one of the most difficult throws in Judo.

(b)   the only known defense for your opponents against that move is to grab your left arm which you don't have."

The above exemplifies that instead of brooding on infirmity, one can always make optimum use of his/her strength. Depending on circumstances even infirmity can turn into an advantage.

8.6   Unlike reasoning, belief has no limit

Believing that something can be done sets the mind in motion to find a way to do it. Wilma Rudolph was born into a poor family in U.S.A in 1940. She was prematurely born and weighed only four and a half pounds. Doctors did not expect her to live. In fact, they were surprised when she lived beyond first few days. At the age of four, she had an attack from double pneumonia and scarlet fever. She was also detected to have been infected by polio. Fighting against death, when she finally recovered, it was noticed that her left leg was crooked and the foot turned inward.

Doctors recommended massage and physical therapy but cautioned and warned that probably Wilma would never walk normal in her life. Her mother however believed at every stage that she would be 'cured' and was determined to try everything to help her daughter.

Rudolph couple was too poor to provide proper medical support to Wilma. Even then, they refused to accept government help.

The mother started treating her at home and occasionally called on doctors only in emergency. She organized four sessions of massages per day to Wilma through her other children. Biweekly, she travelled for an hour by bus to provide Wilma (who was then six years old) treatment in a hospital at Nashville. Wilma had to wear heavy metallic brace to straighten her crooked leg and a heavy brown orthopedic shoe to support her foot.

Though her brothers and sisters were very supportive to her, she was often teased by other kids for her defective leg. This made her very determined to fight against all the odds. She took a resolve that someday 'others' would not only have to accept but also admire her.

At the age of nine, she removed the brace from her leg to try and feel walking like a normal child but on doctors advice she had to use them again. When she reached twelve years of age, her mother packed the brace and sent them back to the hospital in Nashville.

Beating all odds, Wilma finally started walking like a normal child. She however was not satisfied. She set her heart to excel in athletics.

At the age of thirteen, she started participating in various athletic competitions. Finally, at the age of fifteen, she came in touch with Ed Temple. The coach was moved by her spirit and self-confidence and immediately recognized a potential champion in her. Under his training, she put in extraordinary hard work and kept on improving her performance. At the age of sixteen, she represented U.S.A in Melbourne Olympics and won a bronze medal. After four years, she surprised the whole world by winning three gold medals for U.S.A in 1960 Rome Olympics (100 m. sprint, 200 m. sprints and 4 x 100 m. relay).

The story of Wilma Rudolph exemplify that reasoning has limits, but belief has none.

8.7 Quiet submission to divine power

Divine Power plays purposefully and created the following to teach virtues to the mankind for the betterment of the quality of human life.

Earth and stone: to make people understand and learn about stability.

Water: to help people learn about flexibility and persistence. It also teaches mankind, the power in softness and victory in yielding.

Fire: to help people to understand and learn warmth and illumination in broader sense.

Air: to help people to learn 'acceptance and absorption'.

Sky: to glimpse the boundless in it and to understand and learn how to break away from self-imposed limitations.

After exhausting all the avenues of persuasions in any effort, a time comes almost in the life of everyone when he/she quietly submits to divine power for His blessings and guidance believing that nothing happens that He does not permit, and He does not permit anything that does not end well. People perceive the existence of divine power on faith.

Irrespective of whether one calls divine power as Almighty, God, 'a force beyond us' or 'a power much greater than we human being', history reveals that many great men derived inspiration from their belief in divine power.

Mahatma Gandhi once said, "One who has any faith in God should be ashamed to worry about anything whatsoever."

While receiving the award for businessman of the year in 2000, Azim Premji, the CEO of WIPRO, said, "......the most important facilitator of the success is the blessing of a force beyond us.

We can call it luck, we can call it God. As a nonreligious man I attribute much of my success to 'a force beyond me'".

Dr. Walter Staples says, "That a greater intelligence or a higher power exists, there can be no doubt. All the great religion of the world attests to it. Man prides himself on his many accomplishments........but a human being has never created from nothing even a grain of sand, a blade of grass or the leaves of trees. Yet all these things exist. A power much greater than mere human being created them."

8.8 Divine power showers blessings

With limited vision, those who complain about the adversities which they encounter in life should always remember that things might have been worse, if they were not protected by the divine power.

It is said, "When we pray to Almighty, He hears more than we say, He answers more than we ask and He gives more than we imagine but He does everything in His own time and in His own way."

A lone shipwreck survivor on an uninhabited island managed to build a crude hut in which he placed all that he had saved from the sinking ship. He prayed everyday for divine help and scanned the horizon to hail any passing ship. One evening, he was horrified to find his hut in flames. All that he had was gone. He felt that it was the worst that could happen to him and started cursing the Almighty. Yet the very next morning, he was surprised to see a ship anchored close to that area. The captain of the ship came out and told the man, "We have anchored here after seeing smoke signal the previous night to find out if anybody is in distress." The man was rescued.

Though it is a mystery to human beings, irrespective of His 'form' of existence, it is often seen that divine power has a resource for every human need, a definite answer for a human crisis, a definite cure for a human 'hurt' and a guidance for human confusion.

John D. Rockefeller considered to be the richest man in the world during his time, started his career as a clerk earning $3.75 a week out of which he managed to give half of it to God in different forms. When he was fifty-two years of age, he was diagnosed with a serious illness. Doctors told him that he had less than a year to live. While contemplating his own mortality, he derived immense pleasure from his thought of having donated to numbers of organizations including churches etc. He took a resolve to donate his money away on charities. He sold half of his stock in Standard Oil Company and started providing finance to worthy causes all over the world. After few months, he started feeling that something strange was happening to him. The more he gave away, the better he felt! Soon, his doctors checked and declared him free of life threatening illness. He lived till late in his nineties and donated millions and millions of dollars on charities. But the value of his balance of stock in the company appreciated so much that even in his nineties he became richer than what he had at the age of fifty-two years when he started giving his money away.

Wise people rightly say, "Ask God to inspire your thoughts, guide your actions, and ease your feelings. And do not be afraid. God is never wrong."

8.9 Belief sans action is self-deception

Belief inspires and is a driving force. However, simply relying only on belief without doing what needs to be done from time to time can prove to be suicidal.

If one does not do his/her work but still expect everything to happen simply by having belief 'in himself', 'in the world' or 'in divine power', he/she will head for disaster.

Once there was a 'threatening flood' in a small town. For safety, people started moving out of that area. But one man was adamant that he would not leave his house. His belief was, "God will save me, I have faith in him." As the water level rose, a jeep was sent to rescue him. But he refused to move based on his belief that God would save him. As the water level rose further, he went up to the second story. A boat was then sent to rescue him. He again refused to move. The water level kept on rising and the man had to climb to the top of the roof. A helicopter was then sent for his rescue. He refused to accept it based on his belief that God would save him. The water level rose further and the man was ultimately drowned.

8.10 Spirituality stands on belief

Spirituality is 'principled' way of life. Unlike science, where knowledge comes first and belief follows, in spirituality belief comes first then knowledge follows.

Every alphabet of the word 'spirituality' embraces specific attributes which relates to one's thinking and belief on unselfish services for the cause of others.

S stands for Service: S stands for selfless service for others.

P stands for Passage through life: During the passage through life, one needs to follow the philosophy of poet William Penn. He said, "I expect to pass through the life but once, if there be any kindness I can show, let me do it now, as I shall not pass this way once again."

I stand for Integrity: Integrity is steadfast adherence to strict moral and ethical code. It is a concept of consistency of actions, values, methods, principles, measures, expectations and outcomes.

R stands for Restoration: Being restorative makes one think deeply and analyze problems from a broader perspective and find solutions to restore normalcy in life.

I stand for Inner voice: The inner voice guides, directs and helps one to face realities of life in a positive way. It is said, "Your mind only knows something. Your inner voice, your inner instinct knows everything. If you listen to what you know instinctively, it will always lead you down the right path."

T stands for Transcendence: It means being above and independent of material universe with self-control, compassion and realization that the human community is one and indivisible."

U stands for Uniqueness and Oneness of Mankind: This belief enables one to brush aside prejudices and differences so that one can look at others with an open mind.

A stands for Acceptance: Belief and acceptance of 'self' and others unconditionally enables one to negate arrogance with humility. His/her ego therefore remains under control.

L stands for Largeness of Heart: This belief enables one 'to forgive and forget' and always think and do only good to others with focus on the 'present'.

I stand for Inspiration: It is stimulation or arousal of the mind, feelings etc. to special/unusual positive activity or creativity. An inspired person always inspires others.

T stands for Trust and Tranquility: Trust is the reliance on integrity, strength, ability, surety etc. of a person or a thing. With trust, creative thinking and helping hand always stretched towards others, one develops peace of mind and attains tranquility.

Y stands for You (every individual): 'You' signifies that every individual can acquire the above virtues and become a fulfilled person.

Chapter Nine

Conclusions

The awareness of 'dos and don'ts' are very important in life. To emerge as a true winner, there are no short cut routes. Life offers plenty of choices. Zig Zagler rightly says, "The choice one makes determines what he/she will 'have', 'be' and 'do' in the tomorrow of his/her life."

9.1 Ego, anger cause irreparable damage

Ego is a state of awareness where one feels superior to others and wants to exercise power and influence over them.

Ego is self-intoxicating. It is a negative pride that results in arrogance. It has a voracious appetite. The more it is fed, the hungrier it becomes.

Inflated ego causes anger, hatred and clouds one's intelligence to a great extent. Anger is a word which is one alphabet short from the word 'danger'.

Talking about anger Lord Buddha said, "Holding on to anger is like grasping a hot coal with the intent of throwing it to someone else. You are the one who gets burned in the process." Ego and anger make one suffer more than the reason for which one is angry or egoistic.

One day a young boy went to his father and said, "I get angry on slightest pretext and often lose my cool which affects my other activities. Tell me father, what should I do?" The father advised, "Every time you get angry, you hammer a nail in the wooden fence of our back yard." Following father's advice, the boy went on putting a nail on the fence every time he got angry. As time passed, he started realizing that slowly he was able to exercise control on his temper. His frequency of nail hammering into the wooden fence gradually started coming down. After few months, he went to his father again and said, "Father, for last few days I have not lost my temper even once. Now, I am in control of my anger." The father said, "Now, for every day you pass without getting angry, you take out one nail each from the fence." Following that instruction, over a period of time, he took out all the nails from the fence. The boy then went to his father and communicated the development to him. The father expressing his happiness walked along with his son to the site where the nails were hammered. Pointing out towards the impressions left by the nails on the fence he said, "Son! Even though you have controlled your anger, you have not been able to erase its effect on the wall. In our human life too, the impression one sets on the other by expressing anger towards him/her cannot be erased afterwards. This is a hardcore reality."

In the battles of 'ego' and 'anger', irrespective of who wins, one always leaves a scar on the other. Since 'ego' and 'anger' originate from thoughts, one can exercise control on them through conscious efforts.

9.2 Scope for improvement always exists

It is said that human beings use 10/12 per cent of their potential. The famous industrialist Andrew Carnegie had said that average person puts only 25% of his energy and ability into work. The world takes it's hat off to those who put in more than 50% of their capacity and stands on its head for those few and far between souls who devote 100%. It implies from above that there are always scopes for improvement.

Azim Premji, the WIPRO chief, while addressing the students of IIT, Delhi in 2006 said, "Playing to win brings out the best in us and in our teams. It brings out the desire to stretch, to achieve that which seems beyond our grasp. It is about aiming for the maximum, a passion to do our best........ We must remember that no matter how well we do something, there has to be a better way....... Continuous improvement happens when we believe it is possible and when we are willing to work for it. Excellence is not a 'destination' but a journey..................."

In October 2007, the in charge of production and administration of the collieries of Steel Authority of India Limited received a direct phone call from Chairman SAIL on a Saturday afternoon. The chairman asked, "How are things in collieries?" He replied, "We have achieved the monthly target of 70,000 tons of coal which you had set for us in the last SAIL, BOARD meeting." Chairman said, "No, you should make 90,000 tons of production per month." After few months, when the budget for the next year was to be presented to him for his approval, the chairman asked the in charge, "What is your monthly target?" He replied, "90,000 tons/month and also appraised him that in between they had already achieved 90,000 tons of production in one month." Chairman said, "Remake your budget with 100,000 tons of production per month." It was done after thorough review and taking into consideration some of Chairman's promised supports.

Few months later, the Chairman made a visit to the collieries to have first hand interactions with the entire colliery team. Receiving him at Dhanbad railway station and bubbling with confidence, the colliery in charge told him, "Sir, We have achieved 100,000 of production last month. Chairman's cool reply was, "You are capable of achieving 110,000 tons of production every month."

The Chairman thoughtfully stretched the capabilities of the team in steps. The team also responded in affirmative because they were made to believe that they can always achieve more than what had already been achieved by them in the past.

9.3 A bend is not necessarily 'end of that road'

I remember my early career when I joined Indian Iron and Steel Company, Burnpur as an Officer Trainee. After completing the probation period, I was placed in the steel production unit to work in shifts. Steel melting shop then was dominated mostly by people promoted from the ranks and they were resistant to induction of graduate engineers in the shop.

Before my posting in the shop, I was briefed by the Chief of the plant about the 'dos and don'ts. He said, "To make your presence felt in any field, you have to learn the 'specific game' first. Steel melting shop will be just like an unreserved ordinary compartment in Indian railways. Whenever one tries to get in, the passengers from inside tell that there is no place. However, if one can push in, those people ultimately accommodate him/her."

I was inspired. Following his advice, I started learning even from the lowest ranked employees and was gaining in confidence. However, after about a year and a half, I fell into the wrong side of my shift in charge. Situation became so much disturbing and frustrating that I decided to call it quits from steel melting shop. I directly approached the Chief of the plant and requested him to transfer me to some other department.

Assuring me in affirmative, he asked, "If you are changing the department because of X, Y or Z, then remember that you might come across similar personality in other departments too. Would you then again ask for a change?" He further said, "Always be positive. In every walk of life, problems are bound to be there. You must develop the spirit to face and tact to strategize overcoming them."

I got his message. Returning back, I took the resolve that –

(a)   whatever be the circumstances, I shall not succumb to them and run away from steel melting shop as an escapist,

(b)   I shall find my feet on the ground in my own way and create my 'space' to make my presence felt in steel melting shop.

I started working still harder with a change in my thought process and approach towards my boss, peers and subordinates. Few months later, I settled down in steel melting shop as a very trusted lieutenant of the same shift in charge.

Though the above event shook me up initially, it taught me that in the journey in any sphere of life, one is bound to come across bends which are not necessarily the end of that road. One needs to negotiate and maneuver them with thoughtful approaches and careful actions.

9.4 Conclude only after proper assessment

Appearance on first interaction always matters. A painter dressed in dirty worn-out clothes once went to meet Napoleon. Without caring for him, Napoleon asked him to sit in a distant corner. Later after a short conversation, Napoleon came to know that the painter was a master of art and skill. When the painter was leaving, Napoleon got up, walked some distance with him and seen him off as a mark of respect. Before leaving, the surprised painter asked, "Sir, when I came you did not care for me, but now you are showing much courtesy when I am going away!" Napoleon laughed and said, "On arrival, a visitor is judged by his dress. But if he is shown respect on his departure, it is because of his qualities."

I remember my training days in Indian Iron and Steel Company, Burnpur. We were given exposures in different departments in groups (each group consisting of average four trainees). After spending 15 days in each department, the individual group members were interviewed jointly by the heads of training and the concerned department for the assessment of their learning. During training in blast furnace, I did not meet the departmental head, but seeing him in dirty shoes, pant and crumpled shirt (when I appeared for the assessment test), I was thoroughly disappointed. His face was unshaved and hair uncombed. I concluded within myself that he must have been an unqualified man promoted from the ranks by virtue of his seniority in the plant. During interview, when he asked me which book I read on Metallurgical thermodynamics and kinetics, I thought for a while and without any hesitation mentioned O. G. Smith as the author. I was sure that the name would not make any difference to him. He picked up a pencil, struck it few times in his forehead and asked me to spell the name which I did and he let me go. Same evening, I felt ashamed when I came to know that he was not only a doctorate in Metallurgy, he was also a famous Metallurgist of international repute.

Even today, when I recollect the incident, I can clearly remember his face when he was knocking his forehead with the pencil to figure out the book written by O. G. Smith. He must have gone through all the books on Metallurgical Thermodynamics and Kinetics except the one written by O. G. Smith. Actually no such book exists. O. G. Smith incidentally happens to be the name of a late Wet Indian Cricketer.

The above incidents taught me two valuable lessons which I always carry with me.

(a)   Appearance on first interaction always matters, and

(b)   Simply by thinking and concluding without proper assessment that a person is useless or a situation/problem is not worth any attention, one can make a fool of himself/ herself.

9.5 Mind 'diversion' is absolutely essential

I remember accompanying my father to a book fair in late eighties. He purchased few picture posters with captions underneath for his grand children. Returning home, after finishing his distribution of one poster to each child, he was left with one extra which he handed over to me and said, "This one is for you. I have been watching that you are always involved with your plant activities. You don't seem to know that there is a life beyond your 'work' too. Don't be stressed on your plant affairs all the time. Do what needs to be done in your area of work but give rest to your mind and body periodically so that they get time to get recharged. Otherwise, you will become stale."

When I opened the rolled poster, I was emotionally charged. It was the photograph of a young boy in shorts who was sitting on a chair with feet on it and spectacles drooping towards his nose. He was looking towards the 'caption' underneath which read, "I shall not get disturbed unless I disturb myself." The above is very true in human life. People get disturbed only when they allow their mind to get disturbed.

Whether one understands it or not, he/she is always thinking something except when he/she is asleep. This continuous thinking has an adverse impact on the mind and makes a person stale. 'Unwinding' or 'Diversion of mind' therefore, is an absolute necessity in everybody's life. It helps the mind to relax and get back to its natural state. Periodic relaxation relieves stress and makes one fresh, sharper and rejuvenated in spirit.

Leonardo Da Vinci said, "Every now and then go away, have a little relaxation, for when you come back to your work your judgment will be surer. Go some distance away because then the work appears smaller and more of it can be taken in at a glance and a lack of harmony and proportion is more readily seen."

'Diversion of mind' is exercised by different people in different ways. During IPL V in May 2012, Australian fast bowler Brett Lee said to a journalist, "I turn to music during professional problems and personal crisis......... Music provides relief...... Music therapy has been brilliant for me."

Many resort to meditation which is 'cessation of thought process'. It describes a state when one's mind is free from scattered thoughts. Meditation gives rest to the ever working mind so that it can become sharper and a more useful instrument. Meditation does not simply bring about a temporary state of peace and calmness of mind. It is something that is meant to return the mind (which is often not in a stable state due to various sufferings arising out of worries, stress etc.) back to a more natural state of genuine and long lasting peace and well being.

Meditation always needs to be learned under the guidance of a 'Guru'. And the positive effects can only be felt only when the 'practice' is stretched over a considerable period of time.

9.6 Happiness is a conscious decision

There are people who have the tendency to consider their past as better than it really was, present worse than it is and the future less assuring than it will be – as a result they become unhappy. There are also people who believe that happiness is the quotient of one's desires fulfilled divided by the numbers of desires nurtured. However, in reality, fulfillment of a desire does not necessarily lead towards happiness and contentment. With fulfillment of one desire, another desire is born. Disappointment arises when the expectations are not fulfilled.

It is one's feeling towards what he/she has which is important. One can have contentment even with 'little' whereas another person may be discontent with 'much'. That is why it is said that the happiest people do not necessarily have the best of everything; they just make the best of everything. Happiness is self-determining.

Contentment is not an automatic response; it is a conscious decision triggered by certain set of positive attitudes arising out of one's belief, confidence and ability to deal with dislocations and discomforts in life. Abraham Lincoln very candidly said, "Most folks are about as happy as they make up their mind to be."

Happiness does not always depend on doing what one likes or in the fulfillment of expectation of what one likes to have. It depends on one's liking of what he/she does and contentment with what he/she has. External circumstances and relationships can be contributory to happiness but real happiness is determined by the consistency of what one thinks, believes and feels. It is relevant here to quote Mahatma Gandhi. He said, "Happiness is when what you think, what you say and what you do are in harmony."

Dalai Lama said, "The basic thing is that everyone wants happiness, no one wants suffering. And happiness mainly comes from our own attitude rather than from external factors. If your mental attitude is correct, even if you remain in a hostile atmosphere, you feel happy."

9.7 Inspirational event is a driving force

Events have the potential to ignite imagination and inspire people to meet challenges with confidence. Robert Bruce also known as Robert the Bruce, is a national hero of Scotland. He was one of his country's greatest kings and a famous warrior of his generation. Battle after battle (six times) he had led his brave little army and fought with England. Being beaten every time, his army was finally scattered and the king was forced to flee and hide in a cave in the mountains.

One rainy day, Robert the Bruce lay in the cave and was listening to the sound of rainfall outside the cave entrance. He felt dejected, demoralized and sick at heart, and was ready to give up all hope. It seemed to him that there was no use for him to try to do anything more. As he laid thinking, he noticed a spider over his head, getting ready to weave her web. He watched her as she worked slowly and with great care. Six times she tried to throw her thread from one edge of the cave wall to another. Six times her thread fell short. "Poor thing!" said Robert the Bruce, "You, too, know what it is like to fail six times in a row."

But the spider did not lose hope. With still more care, she again got ready to try for a seventh time. Robert the Bruce almost forgot his own troubles as he watched, fascinated. She swung herself out upon the slender line. Would she fail again? No! The thread was carried safely to the cave wall, and fastened there. "Yes" cried Bruce, "I, too, will try a seventh time!"

So, he arose and called all his men to assemble. He told them of his plans, and sent them out with hopeful messages to cheer the discouraged people. Soon there was an army of brave men around him. A seventh battle was fought, and this time the King of England was forced to retreat back to his own country.

Inspiration drawn from the observation of a spider's experience imbibed the spirit of 'fighting for a win' in Robert Bruce who ultimately conquered England in his seventh attempt.

Athlete Florence Griffith Joyner of U.S.A had the privilege to meet Sugar Ray Robinson, the great boxing champion, when she was only eight. During the meeting, Joyner said, "He told me, it does not matter where you come from, what your colour is, or what the odds are against you. What does matter is that you have a dream; you believe you can achieve it and you commit to doing it. It can happen and it will happen.............. Right there, at just eight years of age, I was sold. I was all fired up about what my future could be." The event had a terrific impact on her. She toiled hard, kept her focus on her goal and eventually became the first woman athlete of U.S.A to win four Olympic medals (three gold medals and one silver medal) in the same Olympics (Seoul in 1988).

9.8   Dos and don'ts for successful life

Through her following creation, American author of inspirational poetry, Nancye Sims provides inspirational guidelines to individuals to make the most of life.

A Creed To Live By

Don't undermine your worth by comparing yourself with others.

It is because we are different that each of us is special.

Don't set your goals by what other people deem important.

Only you know what is best for you.

Don't take for granted the things closest to your heart.

Cling to them as you would your life,

for without them, life is meaningless.

Don't let your life slip through your fingers by living in the past or for the future.

By living your life one day at a time,

you live ALL the days of your life.

Don't give up when you still have something to give.

Nothing is really over until the moment you stop trying.

Don't be afraid to admit that you are less than perfect.

It is this fragile thread that binds us each together.

Don't be afraid to encounter risks.

It is by taking chances that we learn how to be brave.

Don't shut love out of your life by saying it's impossible to find time.

The quickest way to receive love is to give;

the fastest way to lose love is to hold it too tightly;

and the best way to keep love is to give it wings.

Don't run through life so fast

that you forget not only where you've been,

but also where you are going.

Life is not a race, but a journey to be savoured each step of the way.

Managing the bosses

Every individual has a boss in his/her place of work and one more at home (spouse). It is absolutely necessary that peace is maintained with both the bosses. When dislocations/problems crop up with the bosses, 'mind' gets disturbed and becomes stressful. Giving vent to relatives and colleagues often does not help in resolving such dislocation/problems. They may listen and sometimes even give advice, but in the long run they start avoiding the person on different pretexts. This is a hardcore reality of life. I have experienced this in my life on many occasions. To deal with the bosses there is no readymade procedure. One has to assess the situations and characteristics of the bosses on case to case basis and respond accordingly. Direct involvement of third persons often does not help in solving such problems.

A wise man rightly said, "Don't tell your personal problems to people; eighty per cent don't care and the other twenty percent are happy that you have them."

Some of the dos and don'ts in life are well hidden in the English alphabets as mentioned below.

'A'lways 'B'e 'C'ool.
'D'on't have 'E'go with 'F'riends and Family.
'G'ive up 'H'urting 'I'ndividuals.
'J'ust 'K'eep 'L'oving 'M'ankind.
'N'ever "O"mit "P"rayers.
'Q'uietly 'R'emember God.
'S'peak 'T'ruth.
'U'se 'V'alid 'W'ords.
'X'press 'Y'our 'Z'eal.

9.9 Attributes of an achiever

Nancye Sims, the American inspirational writer aptly sums up the attributes of an achiever in her following creation.

Winner

Winners take chances like everyone else,
They fear failing, but they refuse to let fear control them.
Winners don't give up,
When life gets tough, they hang in until the going gets better
Winners are flexible.

They realise there is more than one way and they are willing to try others.

Winners know they are not perfect.

They respect their weaknesses while making the most of their strengths.

Winners fall, but they don't stay down.

They stubbornly refuse to let a fall keep them from climbing.

Winners don't blame fate for their failures,

Nor luck for their successes.

Winners accept responsibility for their lives.

Winners are positive thinkers who see good in all things.

From the ordinary, they make the extraordinary.

Winners believe in the path they have chosen even when it's hard,

Even when others can't see where they are going.

Winners are patient.

They know a goal is only as worthy as the effort that's required to achieve it.

Winners are people like you.

They make this world a better place to be.

9.10 Life is full of choices

One is born to live, not live because of being born. Steve Jobs very candidly said, "Your time is limited. So don't waste it living someone else's life. Don't be trapped by dogma – which is living with the results of other people's thinking. Don't let the noise of other's opinions drown out your inner voice. It is important that you have the courage to follow your heart and intuition. They somehow already know what you truly want to become. Everything else is secondary."

Life is full of choices. Like pottery makers shape clay, one can mould and shape his/her life the way he/her desires. Options available are plenty.

One therefore has to be decisive and choose whether he/she should –

(a) be active in setting a goal and sticking to it under all circumstances till the goal is achieved or rely and rest on his/her wishes only?

(b) be enterprising and courageous or choose to play everything safe?

(c) stand by conviction or be guided by inertia?

(d) be led by passion or go through simple motions of life?

(e) capitalize on strengths or concentrate more on shortcomings?

(f) be firm in decision making or be vacillating?

(g) create situations of liking or worry and live with situations even if they are discomforting?

(h) be enthusiastic, optimistic and assertive or avoid facing challenges and embrace self-pity?

(i) look for opportunities to overcome adverse/limiting situations or succumb to them?

(j) be relentless in persuasion or wilt under criticism or any other internal/external pressures?

Zig Zagler rightly says, "You are free to choose, but the choices you make will determine what you will 'have', 'be' and 'do' in the tomorrow of your life."

Detail of Technical Terminologies

All technological terminologies used in the book are explained in this section.

Blast Furnace: It is a counter current vertical shaft furnace. The basic raw materials (iron bearing materials, limestone, dolomite, manganese ore, coke etc.) in solid form are charged from the top. They descend downwards. Preheated air is blown inside the furnace from the bottom and move upwards along with gaseous products of combustion.

Tuyeres: They are water cooled copper members through which air enters the blast furnace. They are positioned above the tap hole.

Hot Metal: They are the main end product of blast furnace operation. They are taken out from blast furnace in liquid form through tap hole provided at the lower part of the furnace. The major percentage of this product is Fe (iron) and the balance contains around 4% carbon, 1% silicon, traces of phosphorous, sulphur, manganese etc. Hot metal is used for making of steel.

Blast Furnace Gases: They are produced inside blast furnace arising out of combustion of solid coke charged by the up going preheated air. They are rich in carbon monoxide and hydrogen. These gases carry physical heat. They exit from the top of the furnace, collected and are used as fuel in steel plants.

Blast Furnace Burden: The down coming solid raw materials charged from the top of the blast furnace consists of measured quantities of iron ore, limestone, dolomite, manganese ore, etc. against fixed amount of coke per charge. This is known as burden. With burden fixed, coke quantity per charge can also be adjusted.

Prepared Burden: Fines of iron ore, limestone, dolomite, coke etc. are also agglomerated in measured quantities to form permeable masses and charged into a blast furnace. Depending on process characteristics, they are either called sinter or pellet. When they are charged with hard coke in measured quantities into a furnace, it is said that the furnace is charged with prepared burden.

Prepared burden is also referred to calculated burden charged during blowing down of a furnace so that subsequent evacuation of the furnace inside becomes easier during dismantling before relining or stack gunning.

The Stack Of The Blast Furnace

It is the inclined top of the blast furnace where the charged materials mostly remain in solid form.

The Bosh Parallel of blast furnace joins the stack with hearth. Here the solid charges start getting marshy before becoming two separate liquids (slag and metal) in the hearth.

Hearth Of A Blast Furnace is the lowest part of the furnace where the liquid metal and slag are held before they are taken out from the furnace.

Partial Relining Of Blast Furnace: It consists of the following steps.

(I)   Charging the furnace with prepared burden with layers of nut coke above the tap hole keeping the top of the furnace empty as far as possible.

(II)   Raking out and shifting the nut coke to a predetermined site.

(III)   Dismantling the bosh parallel.

(IV)   Digging 40 inches around the hearth periphery (up to an approximate depth between the third to fourth courses of the hearth bricks from the top most layers.

(V)   Bricking of hearth wall along with bosh parallel.

(VI) Surface patching of the stack with gunning, if necessary.

The above is carried out essentially to prolong the campaign life of blast furnace with minimum possible investments.

Overburden: Coal is formed in seams. Above the coal seams there are layers of soil, rock and other materials which need to be removed before the coal can be extracted. These layers are known as overburden.

Overburden is removed after drilling and blasting of waste rock till the coal seams are exposed. The overburden thus removed is stacked in an identified area which can subsequently be used for various purposes like filling of low land etc. Coal thus exposed is recovered.

Open Cast Mining: There are two basic methods of coal extraction ---open cast mining and underground mining.

Open cast mining is used when the coal lies at a reasonable depth from the surface. Underground mining can go to a depth of even more than 400 meters from the surface (Jitpur colliery of SAIL, India). In underground mining, either vertical shaft or incline method is adopted for extracting coal.

Viability of coal extraction by any method is determined by coal to overburden ratio, quality as well as quantity of coal reclaimable and economy of transporting overburden as well as coal to identified stock yards.

Coke Ovens: Coke is produced by heating of coal out of contact with air in coke ovens.

It is through the side walls of each oven that the coal mass receives the heat. The heat finally proceeds toward the centre to make the coke.

Coke: Coke has high energy value which is released when its fixed carbon reacts with oxygen of the hot air inside the blast furnace. Depending on size, various fractions of coke are known as blast furnace coke, nut coke, pearl coke etc.

Coke Oven Gas: Gases generated during the process of carbonization in coke oven is known as coke oven gas. They have high calorific value and are reclaimed and used as fuel in steel plants.

Decoaled Area: The areas in coalfield from the underneath of which coal have been extracted and is filled up with sand or any other filler materials is known as decoaled area.

Open Hearth Furnaces: These are front doors charged horizontal furnaces where steel is made from either liquid metal or scrap or from both in identified proportions. Fuel is fired through burners from either side of the furnace hearth alternately and the final steel is tapped through a tap hole provided at the backside of the furnace. It works on regenerative chequer systems where the sensible heat of the outgoing gases (from the fuel combustion as well as from the chemical heat of reaction from the hearth) are utilized for heating the chequer bricks which pre heats the combustion air. These furnaces have low productivity and fuel utilization.

Top Air/oxygen Lancing: When jets of air through lances over the open hearth furnace roofs are used to accelerate the reaction kinetics of the steel making process, it is called top air lancing. When oxygen from top is utilized for agitation, the process is called top oxygen lancing.

Heat Load In Open Hearth Furnace: It is the total thermal load arising out of combustion of fuel fired and chemical heat of reactions in the hearth chamber.

Metallurgical Load: It is the total metallic and gangue material charged into the furnace hearth.

Twin Hearth Furnaces: These furnaces are similar to the open hearth furnaces with the following differences:

1. The hearth is having a baffle wall creating two separate hearths.

2. There is no regenerating chequer brick system in the flue.

3. No additional fuel is fired through the burners during operation (there are provisions for usage of fuel from the top for initial heating of the furnace system).

4. When one hearth is refining, the other hearth is charged with cold material. The waste gases from the refining chamber during their way out through the chimney heat the cold stock of the second chamber. The same sequence is followed in the reverse cycle.

They are generally fixed type unlike open hearth furnaces which can either be fixed or tilting type. Compared to open hearth furnaces, Twin hearth furnaces have higher productivity and are easy to maintain with no support of external fuel required.

Full Roof/short Roof Repair: Generally every alternate campaign repair of twin hearth furnace requires full roof to be replaced. In the mid campaign repairs only few rings in the middle of the roof are replaced (along with bricking of the front and back wall). Such campaign repairs are known as short roof repair.